Living With Vision:

Reclaiming the Power of the Heart

by Linda Marks

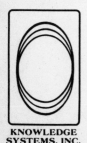

**KNOWLEDGE
SYSTEMS, INC.**

Published by Knowledge Systems, Inc.
7777 West Morris Street, Indianapolis, Indiana 46231

Printed in the United States of America

First Edition
ISBN 0-941705-07-2

About the Book

From this book you can expect to:

Empower the visionary in you. In truth, no one can empower anyone else. You can only empower yourself. However, the ideas, exercises, and stories in this book provide a mirror in which you can see parts of yourself you might have forgotten or have not taken seriously.

Give voice and credence to the wisdom of your heart. Our times call for more than information, analysis and intellect, but our culture tends to revere the mind and discredit the heart. While the mind is powerful enough to create whatever it imagines, only the heart knows what really matters.

Acknowledge the place of working with your dark side. Our culture will pay any price for comfort, telling us pain is something to be avoided or gotten rid of. We are terrified of the unknown, by anger, grief and other "negative" feelings, and by the darkness of the night. The dark side is part of the cycle of life. Opening yourself to the dark side, you will discover how obstacles are transformed as you face and embrace them and discover your own wholeness and depth.

Achieve a clear understanding of vision and develop a set of tools to live with vision as an individual. Through practical exercises and people's stories you will see how you can make your mark and how others are making theirs. You'll learn how to live with vision in your daily life and bring your unique gifts to relationships, your work, and the organizations you are part of. You'll be able to explore your unique contribution and where you fit in the larger scheme of things.

Find a way to return to nature and learn ways of living that are sustainable today and tomorrow. This includes both your own nature as a human being and the world around you. Many models in the text are taken from nature.

To my children, who are yet to be born,
and to all of our children
and our children's children.
May it nurture the spark of life that lives inside us all
and help create a loving, peaceful,
sustainable world today and tomorrow.

Table of Contents

Foreword

I welcome this book, both as a deeply personal statement and as a powerful tool for those wishing to explore their deeper purposes and change their lives for the better. The first step, I have found, is to become more aware of ourselves and re-acquaint ourselves with our pristine, natural idealism and our earliest dreams and visions.

Linda Marks tells us of her own journey toward wholeness and the lessons she learned along the way. In today's world of shifting values, changing paradigms and widespread cultural confusion, we become wary of the old leadership and the old prescriptions. We need more heartfelt personal witnessing. We want to learn from those who walk their talk. Linda Marks' commitment to share her life's experience with others makes this book both a pleasure and a treasure of useful information.

I found myself comparing my own journey with Linda's and enjoying the similarities. I too, was a very determined little girl—quite sure that my joy in myself, my awareness and the magical beauty of the natural world around me was the birthright of every member of the human family. I, too, found that the daily "realities" I was often urged to accept—pain, suffering, hunger, wars, pollution and destruction of the Earth—were unacceptable to me. I knew that they must be changed if the human family was to survive. At a very young age, I too, vowed that my life would be about trying to change things for the better—although I had no idea how. Those counselling me to adapt, fit in or go along with the way things were, simply made me feel more and more like an extraterrestrial. This vision of having arrived on a strange planet stayed with me for many years—even as I learned all of the behavioral repertoires that would allow me to understand various human cultures and communicate with my sisters and brothers on this magnificent planet. This book will help widen and deepen human dialogues about what is truly valuable and important and what we need to learn together about our situation as a five-billion member human family.

Many others began this dialogue as I did, by banding together with others to try to prevent further environmental destruction and pollution. I started on the problem "out there" and in so doing learned slowly but surely the ecologists' truth about the interconnectedness of everything. Environmental pollution could not be understood without understanding human cultures, behaviors, politics, economics, and the way all of them related to natural systems and cycles. I soon learned to look inward and realize how much more I needed to know about myself and my own motives, vision, pain and joy. I came to understand that we can only heal ourselves and, by doing this well, help in healing the planet.

I gradually focused in on systems theory and decision-making around all the momentous technological choices which humans were making with life or death implications. I was and still am motivated by the need to address the age-old question, "What is valuable?" under radically changing conditions of globalization and planetary interdependence. I decided to try to unravel the hidden assumptions and rationalizations of economics—from left to right—which seemed to have such a strange-hold on public policy, business decisions and our personal choices, including the massive confusions created about money, which was no longer a useful invention for measuring but had become reified as a commodity as if it had intrinsic worth. Linda Marks shares my interest in revealing the difference between money and wealth.

After twenty years of studing economics, I came to see this discipline and all its various schools of thought—from Karl

Marx and Adam Smith, Keynes and the "supply-siders" favored by Ronald Reagan—is but a clouded and distorted set of spectacles which obscures, rather than enlightens, today's debate about what is valuable. That which economists have taught us to view as an "economy" can never be abstracted from its social, political and ecological context. Thus its axioms and theories are suspect and often revealed as loaded with a priori assumptions, skewed by the values of economists themselves and little more than politics in disguise.

Instead, I came to view "economies" as sets of rules laid down by the various values, customs, laws and goals of different cultures so as to operationalize those value systems. In other words, far from being peripheral, values are the key variable that drives both technological and economic systems. It is for this reason that this book focuses on clarifying values; not only can this help us clarify our personal lives and purposes, but it is these value-systems which are the collective "cultural DNA" of any society. As I have elaborated elsewhere, we now need scientists and economists to give up the pretense to "value-free objectivity" in their work, so that the value-dimensions of all human activities can be explored and debated freely.

The massive changes our planet is undergoing today are largely the result of prior human interventions guided by short-term values, inadequate understanding, and disfunctional beliefs and ideologies. Six great globalization processes have been unleashed: 1) the globalization of technology and production; 2) of finance, economic systems and debt; 3) the arms race; 4) pollution and environmental depletion; 5) work, employment and migration; and 6) the globalization of consumption and the emergence of a global culture. Thus countries are re-structuring and re-aligning themselves and their domestic institutions, and this process is creating ever-greater levels of uncertainty and disruption in the lives of every one of us. Many of us perceive, correctly, that it may be actually safer to jump out of our existing life patterns and strike out for something closer to our hearts' desire than to stand pat and risk being overwhelmed by change. At such times, the best recourse for all of us is to look inward, revive our long-lost dreams and desires, clarify our values, and learn to embrace and even ride the tiger of change. At the same time, never has the role of imagination and the ability to envision creative, alternative futures been more crucial to our species. This book can be a companion in your personal adventure.

HAZEL HENDERSON
Anastasia Island
St. Augustine, Florida
July, 1988

Introduction

For a long time I have been convinced that each one of us has a gift to give the world, a unique message or contribution. Throughout the course of our lives, we find different forms and different ways to give this gift, to express this message. In this sense, I have been writing and living this book all my life, in poetry, in songs, in business, in relationships, in what I've done, in who I am.

My attempt to live with vision has not been easy, nor often understood by others, but has meant going against the grain of society, being different, and often having that which is sacred to me neither valued nor rewarded. Recently the climate has been changing. There is a search for meaning in our lives, a recognition that the future is in our hands, a realization that who we are and how we live is what really matters. We are in a new stage in our evolution as human beings in which vision is an essential tool of change.

While more and more people are beginning to recognize that vision is essential, what it is and how to live with it seem elusive. Vision is little understood, difficult to grasp, and even harder to sustain over time through encounters with seemingly overwhelming obstacles. "Yes, it's important, but how do I live with vision?" becomes the question in our hearts and minds. We feel small next to the people who serve as models. "Sure Einstein and Kennedy had visions, but they were extraordinary individuals." There is a myth that visions must be large and superhuman in order to be valid. A limited understanding of vision disempowers us.

Actually, vision is a capacity within every person on Earth. Most people want to live powerful, creative and purposeful lives. What often stops us from making our own unique contribution is not believing this is possible, not knowing where we fit in the scheme of things, not knowing how to use what we have. This book is intended to show that a sustainable future can be created, that each of us can make a difference, and each of us can make a mark on the world by being who we truly are.

When I was 14, I wrote the following lines:

> *A thin line stands between dream and reality*
> *And only the heart knows the characteristics*
> *That correspond to either side.*

This poem, appeared under the picture in my high school yearbook and captures my childhood experience of finding life confusing. Like most children, I was told by adults that the apparent craziness in the world was "reality," the way I knew things *could* be, idle fantasy. They said "dreams" and "reality" had no relationship to one another. "Reality" was something that held us victim or hostage forever. "Reality" had been there before we were born and certainly was going to remain long after our deaths. This thought made no sense and I felt sad and powerless.

I was filled with dreams and creative energy. Dreams lived in my heart and fueled my passion. Dreams compelled me to act. I saw how they could be made real through choice, commitment and action. Dreams weren't separate from reality but were roadmaps to create new realities. They were a kind of pre-reality. Was the world backwards, or was I simply a kid with wild ideas? While confused, I believe I really knew the answer.

Even as a child I would ask myself, "What is really important? What really matters to me? What feels true in my heart of hearts?" As the answers developed, sometimes slowly, sometimes quickly, I would then ask, "How can I find a way to act on what matters? What can I do? Where can I find the resources I need? How can I create what I truly want?" Either out of naivete, or perhaps wisdom, I would then act on the answers received.

Learning About Vision: My Own Experience

Looking back on my childhood, I realize that what I was discovering was the process of living with vision. People are by nature creative. Vision, our capacity to craft new possibilities, lives in our hearts and evolves over time. Living with vision leads us into the unknown, makes new frontiers our home, and enables each of us to be a leader and an architect even if often we feel vulnerable or don't know all the answers. I'd like to share an experience that taught me much about living with vision.

Having a piano was important to me as a child. Music beat in my heart and bones. As a toddler, I was attracted to the piano and found myself learning to play simple tunes quite naturally. At my grandfather's house, I sneaked off and sounded out the notes to "Oh Christmas Tree" on the piano with great enthusiasm and determination. I was embarrassed by my passion for the piano. "We don't want children banging on the piano," my grandfather would say. "I'm not banging," I would think. "I'm making it sing!" My family did not have a piano and greeted my continuous requests for one with answers like, "We can't afford a piano. Why don't you learn to play another instrument?" Or "Music is a waste of a good mind." I felt hurt by their responses. Couldn't my parents see how important the piano was to me? My great-grandfather had a piano that he promised to me but then gave to someone else. I felt betrayed.

"If I want a piano, I have to find another way," I concluded. At first an eight-year-old friend had promised to teach me to play. She was a young entrepreneur who charged me for the lessons. After a while these lessons felt like an act of commerce rather than an act of love. Besides, I couldn't practice whenever I wanted. I needed to have a piano of my own—there for me when I felt the impulse. I began to find ways a little girl could earn money—selling lemonade, painting rocks to sell on the street corner, saving money from birthday gifts and holidays, earning money from my parents for good grades at school. I did whatever I could. Through considerable effort and perseverance, by the time I was thirteen, I had saved up $350. One evening I walked into the living room and told my parents, "Drive me to the store. I want to buy my piano." Realizing I was serious, they took me to the store and, at last, I had my piano.

All the way along the path, my efforts to express the music inside of me were impeded by obstacles. When I look back, however, what I remember is that the desire to express the songs in my heart was so compelling that, no matter what the obstacle, I kept moving forward. Although lacking the words to describe what I was doing as a child, I followed the vision in my heart and made it happen.

One final point in the piano story. I consider music to be a metaphor for my work in the world: living with vision, listening to my heart, and being used as an instrument for a higher purpose.

Making a Difference:
Living With Vision and Personal Purpose

While some of the things I learned related to my own growth, many reached beyond the realm of self. I have always wanted to contribute, to make the world a better place. Pen pals around the world introduced me to different cultures and enabled me to see underlying similarities.

The civil rights movement, people starving in Biafra, and the senseless deaths of many people in Vietnam affected me deeply. I remember singing with conviction, "Let there be peace on Earth and let it begin with me." I cried singing the words to "Abraham, Martin and John." I kept asking, "Why can't we treat one another with respect and dignity? Why is there such violence in our society?" My questions and relentless curiosity scared many people.

It was painful to live in a world that said what really mattered to me was futile and foolish. I felt sad and alone, as if I did not belong here. Martin Luther King, John F. Kennedy, and Robert Kennedy were assassinated before my eyes while pursuing their dreams. I was scared and did not want to die violently. Still, I had an unusual amount of violence in my early life. I spent the first sixteen years struggling with the choice of whether to live or die. I considered suicide at 8, attempted suicide at 12, became anorexic at 13. At 16, I was attacked by a stranger while walking home from work and was almost murdered. What I realize now is that the violence I experienced was a mirror of a struggle going on inside me. Did I have the courage to really live, to be who I truly was? I was afraid of living fully, of taking my place in the world, of truly being who I was.

In the course of the attempted murder, I confronted the fundamental issue of living or dying and faced my fear. It was a profound turning point in my life. In coming so close to death, I realized what a gift life is—to be treasured, savored and honored. The time had come to get on with my life, to live and become what I had always known I could be. Since that time, while I often have doubted myself, I have never doubted my mission. I had been afraid of death. Death seems unimportant now. I was given something that went so deep and felt so powerful that I knew this awareness would never leave me. And that conviction, that choice, has moved me through great pain and accomplishment, times of clarity and times of not knowing, both consciously and unconsciously.

As I hope to illustrate in this book, the strength, clarity and commitment that come from facing the darkness is a foundation for living with vision. Vision is the foundation on which we can create what really matters for ourselves, for others and for humanity. At a time when our old models, methods and structures are breaking down and failing, at a time when we are faced with the destruction of our natural environment, with the ability to destroy life itself through nuclear war, we need new possibilities. Never before have we needed such clarity of vision.

Finding a Way to Make a Mark: My Own Journey

It has taken most of my 30 years to really learn what living with vision means. Learning how to integrate the three major threads of my life—medicine or healing, business, and art or music—has been a slow process.

I have always known I was a healer. Medical careers run in my family. I have always had an interest in the mind-body connection, particularly in relationship to cancer and heart disease. In the 1970s, I discovered the world of Lawrence LeShan, Kenneth Pelletier, and Carl and Stephanie Simonton. I knew they were on the right track. I considered a traditional medical career, worked briefly in medical research and realized this was not my path. For me, the medical world was about curing illness not cultivating wellness. My greatest interest was in preventive medicine—recognizing the relationship between wellness and disease, learning how to live well and so not need to get sick. Over the years I have found that illness is an invitation to reclaim our wholeness, an invitation to grow, learn and live a purposeful life.

I was greatly impacted by the work of Hans Selye, by his important book *The Stress of Life*. His understanding of the relationship between wellness and personal purpose particularly struck me. He acknowledged that the little irritations of daily life, the way we live from moment to moment, contribute more to our stress level than major life crises. The greatest sources of negative stress are a sense of waste, futility or purposelessness.

In 1979 I entered the world of business. I felt it was more honest than the worlds of medicine, music and education, because in business economic issues did not have to be camouflaged but could be talked about pragmatically without guilt. I was struck by the separation of profit and service motives in our culture and saw business as a place to try to integrate the two. I searched to find a company that cared about people whose values were compatible with my own. I did not know if I could find one.

Ironically, it was my link to the medical community that led me to find a company I could be proud of. An administrator at the hospital where I had done research introduced me to a friend who worked for Digital Equipment Corporation. Digital was a company that valued people and creativity. I entered the corporate world in a novel capacity: as a staff person to a senior management task force looking at strategic issues for the next decade. I became a consultant without even knowing what one was and, because I didn't know any better, did a stellar job and kept getting hired back.

Being practical, recognizing that my undergraduate studies in music and psychobiology at Yale had little value in the corporate world, I pursued a graduate management degree at the Sloan School of Management, MIT. I continued my special relationship with Digital, working part-time on an innovative organization development project. As always happened with me, a small project blossomed into a major change effort. It finally brought together people from five different business units and many levels within the organization to develop a program that empowered many people and received corporate attention.

While working in the business world I also pursued my artistic and medical interests. I studied wholistic medicine, learning a variety of healing methods incorporating mind, body and spirit. I was a singer/songwriter, performed in the Boston area and cut a tape of original music in 1983. I founded the Boston Arts Roundtable, a nonprofit organization providing support for artists of different genres and producing multi-media concerts.

While I seemed to have everything—a significant love relationship, a successful career, a rich assortment of outside activities, in 1984 I realized I needed to make a change. My life was divided into a series of compartments. I wanted to integrate my life. I realized the scope of my work was still limited. One corporation was both too small and too large an arena for me to work in. I wanted to work globally with many people and organizations and intimately with individuals, facilitating their healing, self-discovery and, ultimately, happiness.

In 1985 I made major changes in my life all at once. I broke off my engagement, left the corporate world and jumped into the unknown, making a full commitment to live with vision and do the work I was meant to do from the very beginning.

I have learned there are many ways to make a difference, to express my vision. Today my work has many forms:

As a healer, I'm a body-centered psychotherapist, helping clients explore the relationship of mind and body in illness, wellness and quality of life.

As an artist, I'm a writer of songs, articles and books,

finding ways to express the unspeakable and to share with others the learning of my heart.

As a teacher and a guide, I lead workshops and give talks nationally and globally, reaching a wide variety of people in a wide variety of settings. More informally I play my part, being me, wherever I show up in the world.

As a consultant and facilitator of social evolution, I work with individuals, organizations, and groups of social visionaries committed to creating sustainable ways of living and working today and tomorrow.

As a social entrepreneur, with my business partner Wynne Miller, I run a company called the Marks-Miller Collaborative offering workshops on Money, Work and Personal Purpose, helping individuals and organizations make a difference while making a profit and putting into practice the philosophy and methods we offer to others. I am a co-founder, with Susan Meeker-Lowry, of the Institute for Gaean Economics, which is exploring ways to apply natural principles to the care and management of all the Earth's resources. Over the years, I have founded and co-founded many organizations, responding to the needs of the time, particularly in the areas of art and business.

This book is part of my vision. It is a means of reaching people, contributing to the quality of life, touching people I may not meet in my travels. Ten percent of the proceeds I receive from this book are being used to seed the Living With Vision Foundation, supporting people in living from their hearts and making a contribution to the greater good.

I have learned that while the marketplace may value my many skills differently, for me they are equally valuable. I need to balance the use of my skills to feel whole and complete. I seek quality in my life and integration.

I have learned more in the three and a half years since my leap into the unknown than I have in the rest of my lifetime. Many lessons have been hard and painful — in love, business, friendships and my understanding of myself. Too, I've been given gifts and opportunities in all parts of my life that have touched me deeply and will stay with me forever. Today I feel that I am really living my purpose, contributing to society and the quality of life on Earth.

I hope this book can be a mirror of discovery that helps you remember the things you've always known and perhaps had forgotten. It will give you an understanding of vision and how it relates to our place in human evolution, techniques to unearth your sense of personal purpose through clarifying what really matters, support for the wisdom of your heart as you learn to embrace the dark side of life, and tools to help you manage the many resources inside your body.

I offer this book to you with love, hoping it provides you with some small insight, new tool, or source of inspiration which supports you in living fully, knowing your place in the larger scheme of things and working in partnership with others to create a world we will be proud to pass on to our children's children.

PART 1

Finding
Your
Vision

CHAPTER 1

Reclaiming Our Wholeness

*I don't know what your destiny will be,
but one thing I do know:
the ones among you who will be really happy
are those who have sought and found how to serve.*
— *ALBERT SCHWEITZER*

Humanity is arriving at a new point in evolution. From a developmental point of view, we could call it the coming into adulthood of our species. As adults, as conscious/compassionate people having established a sense of personal identity we are beginning to recognize that all beings are both unique individuals and a part of nature. Each of us is part of a common living system with distinct roles to play and a common purpose: the full expression of life. We are interdependent and interrelated in the healthiest sense. Creative power, we are learning, is a natural resource enabling us to work in partnership with nature. And we are discovering that while we are not ultimately in control we can affect our destiny.

In this critical phase in human evolution, as life's higher purpose is becoming clearer, we are being challenged to change our structures and ways of life to serve this larger purpose. Service includes both our desire to express ourselves, to give our gift in order to fully experience our vitality and sense of self, and our desire to contribute selflessly to a greater good. Often we feel these two aspects are mutually exclusive: how can one both nourish oneself and give self-lessly? I ask how they cannot be interrelated. You can only give to others when you feel you have something to give. Self-care and service go hand in hand.

Indeed, the very nature of life today calls for a vision of wholeness. We are searching for ways to bridge the splits between mind and body, ourselves and nature, ourselves and others. In this book, I invite you to join me on a journey into the nature of life and the nature of your life.

The Need for Vision

In today's world, nothing seems constant but change. The rate of change accelerates daily. New technology, more and more information, and seemingly endless options characterize our times. Innovations may provide advantages, but the speed of change accentuates the fragmentation, lack of focus, and broken relationships so characteristic of our time. Often we feel incomplete and inadequate, afraid to trust our own capability and experience. In this sense, innovation is working against our need for integration.

Change can be freeing, opening doors never imagined possible; change also can be overwhelming as we try to absorb ever increasing amounts of complex information. While we may try to know everything, to do so becomes stressful. Our lives challenge us to build order out of chaos or surrender to forces beyond our control.

No matter how quickly I read, my work space is constantly adorned with stacks of correspondence to be answered, publications to be read, even mail to be sorted through. I once prided myself on managing the flow of information that came across my desk efficiently. Those days are long gone. The volume of paper and information that comes in the door is too great. A look at the stacks overwhelms me.

I don't like living with chaos, yet to keep on top of the growing paper piles would take most of my time several days a week. A few years ago, I decided to act by limiting the flow of paper. I stopped receiving the local newspaper and cancelled most of the periodicals I subscribed to. While afraid that I would lose touch with the "real world," the practical part of me realized that the publications were seldom read.

Still, for all my effort and good intention, the flow of paper has not lightened. What I have learned, though, is to accept the fact that I can't possibly keep up with all the information out there and that being frustrated doesn't serve me. These days, I listen more often to my intuition that tells me when to turn on the radio or buy a newspaper. Observing how information manages to find its way to me, whether from a friend, an associate or even a total stranger, is eye-opening.

The pace and style of modern life also breeds separation. As we move through the pace of our busy workday, we find ourselves on solitary paths. Others are just as busy so finding time to spend with those we care about and even finding others we truly want to be with becomes difficult. One day I came to a sobering realization. "How much time do you actually get to spend with your friends?" I asked myself. "How many relationships consist in talking on the phone or even to one another's answering machines?" My friends are caring, but they too are busy people. Elaborate calendar planning is necessary to get together.

This separation is not only from one another, but also from ourselves. Our lives appear to be endless treadmills. We are good at being productive and efficient but are stressed out, tired and caught in a way of living that leaves no space to breathe. We don't have time to stop and reflect on what we are doing, where we are going and whether or not that's the direction we really want to take.

As you struggle through your day and week, do you pause to ask yourself what you really want, what you truly care about, what you need? Or is your life reduced from living to surviving? Is life primarily a struggle to maintain your footing and equilibrium? Have you lost a sense of joy?

What is happening around the world does not make life easier. Faced with the threat of nuclear annihilation, a breakdown in the world monetary system, the spread of the AIDS epidemic, inadequate political leaders and the rapid destruction of the Earth's resources, we feel even more powerless. These problems seem so urgent, so overwhelming, how can one individual possibly make a dent? We all feel powerless and insignificant in light of what needs to be done.

In trying to meet the challenges, our old ways of thinking and acting are coming up empty. A generation ago "having it all" meant getting the job, the house, the car, the family, living in a nice neighborhood and saying "I've done it." There is a price paid for this kind of "success." Even those who choose to pay the price and "do it right" feel something is lacking. "Having a good job" is adequate no longer. We yearn for something more. Sex roles and relationships between men and women are confusing. When we try to play a traditional part, something's missing. Our hunger for community goes unfulfilled.

We long to feel connected to ourselves and to others. In our hearts we yearn for fulfillment, for peace and for community. "Is it even possible to fulfill this longing?" we wonder. What can one hold on to when beliefs, methods and institutions no longer provide answers? Where do we go? What do we do? Today we are asking ourselves questions about the very meaning, nature and purpose of life.

The Personal Journey

When I was a little girl, I sometimes thought life was some giant's dream and people were all characters in his imagination. Walking around self-absorbed in our own stories and dramas, we took ourselves terribly seriously while the giant watched us flitting about and laughed and laughed.

In many ways, this image provides a good metaphor for how we live our lives. We are often so caught up in our personal drama we forget that we are part of a larger context—part of a world, part of a species called humanity, and part of the constantly changing drama called life. When seen in isolation, our personal drama may seem pointless, our circumstances unfair and our efforts futile. At times we may even question the meaning of life.

Somewhere deep inside, however, I think most of us know that life is purposeful. We know there's got to be more than the drudgery of daily tasks; there has to be some method to what often only seems to be madness. There is a hunger, a yearning, a craving to find a sense of purpose, a sense of deeper meaning in life and in our lives. With this yearning comes a boundless curiosity: a desire to learn, to grow, to explore, and to discover.

As children, this curiosity came naturally. We asked a lot of questions. We found pleasure in asking why. We saw ourselves as explorers, students and dancers to the music of life. Somehow as we grew up our curiosity got stifled, shut off or buried. We were told to stop asking so many questions, to mind our own business and to accept commonly held beliefs as the truth. We turned off our curiosity and with it our passion, until later in life accidents or personal crises forced us to confront and question the way we lived and what we believed.

These crises mark the beginning of what can be called "the personal journey." In this journey we seek to discover if there is indeed greater meaning in life and, if so, where we fit in the larger picture of things. We want a clearer understanding of the nature of life and the purpose for our own lives.

The Need to Know

I have a favorite poem that Ranier Maria Rilke wrote.

> *Be patient with all that is unresolved in your heart*
> *And try to love the questions themselves*
> *Do not seek for the answers that cannot be given*
> *For you would not be able to live them*
> *And the point is to live everything*
> *Live the questions now*
> *And perhaps without knowing it*
> *You will live along some day*
> *Into the answers.*

Whenever I read this poem, my heart recognizes the truth of Rilke's words. In practice, however, I have many days when I find it hard, even frustrating, to live with questions and uncertainty. Human beings have a great need to know. When I don't know, I feel anxious, insecure, uncomfortable and very vulnerable. The world places a high value on knowledge, as though if you "knew it all," you then would be omnipotent, secure and free from the natural cycles, the highs and lows that you and everyone experiences. In this sense the "Age of Reason," the worship of the rational mind, has become an imprisoning monster.

Knowledge, we are taught, is something we lack and have to acquire. We gather information from experts, computers, books, universities and authorities, all outside sources of knowledge. Knowledge is something we gather and store in our minds. Then when we are faced with uncertainty our minds become the authority that helps us feel in control. We look to our minds for answers and understanding. When we don't know something we analyze, quantify, judge, and rationalize, trying to figure it out, to find the answer, to find meaning. We were taught that if we were smart enough, if we did it right, we always would come up with *the answer*.

It could be said that in our culture we live in our heads, as though the head were not connected to the rest of the body. While feeling in control of oneself may feel secure, the price we often pay is the loss of our natural resources and capacities. Our hearts, intuition, instincts, and dreams are buried or forgotten as we consider only rational information. Maintaining this kind of control can lead us to feel incomplete and isolated. How can anyone feel full, whole and connected when cut off from so much of oneself?

There are many times in life when there is no *right* way to do things or be in control. Try as we may to figure things out, to understand, there are no pat answers. Wracking our brains only brings headaches. At such times we feel angry and frightened as though we were up against a wall, a wall in front and inside ourselves. As we feel trapped we begin to ask, "Is there something I don't see? Is there another way to look at things?"

Knowing and Evolving

This way of living is from a rational or linear point of view. However looking at ourselves from an evolutionary perspective[1] enables us to understand both why we feel such a need to know and be in control and also why such a viewpoint does not feel right or complete. We are moving from a phase in our evolution where we viewed ourselves as separate from nature and in control of life to a phase where we are rediscovering our partnership with nature and our part in the dance of life.

The evolutionary process perhaps can be understood best as the swing of a pendulum from one extreme to another extreme way of being. We are now in the process of moving to the center and finding a point of integration and balance between the two. The extreme swings of the pendulum in our evolution I call "the primal stage" and "the thinking stage." The place in the center I call "the conscious/compassionate stage." (See Diagram 1:1)

THE EVOLUTIONARY SPIRAL

Primal   Thinking   Conscious/
Stage   Stage   Compassionate
                                  Stage

DIAGRAM 1:1

The Primal Stage

Looking back to humanity's roots, our first ancestors seem to have experienced themselves as part of nature. Like newborn children, they did not yet have a separate personal identity or an independent sense of self. Nature was both parent and creator, experienced as all-powerful and all-knowing. People then felt vulnerable to nature's power; survival focused on the natural forces that could not be controlled. In this phase of human evolution the concept of God was *God as nature*, representing forces in the environment.

The Thinking Stage

In the thinking stage we humans developed an understanding of the world 180 degrees opposite to that of primal people. Like adolescents we needed to develop a separate identity, to differentiate ourselves from nature and from others. We sought control over our own destiny and control over nature. We wanted to be all-powerful and all-knowing, to develop the power of our minds. The world we created insulated us from many of the forces of nature. We looked at nature primarily as a provider of needed resources. In this phase of evolution we created God in our own image— a knowing, judging God who determined right and wrong, and maintained control over life. God was an authority figure—one we feared, respected and, at times, rebelled against.

The Conscious/Compassionate Stage

As we reach adulthood, the conscious/compassionate stage, we are being asked to integrate our sense of self with our place in nature and the larger purpose of life. We are coming to a new understanding of our creative power, reclaiming the heart and linking it with the mind. When our thoughts and actions are conscious and in harmony with nature's sense of timing, the natural order of things, we become co-creators. We are coming to a new understanding of God as a creative force or capacity that resides inside all human beings. This God is all-seeing and all-knowing, asking us to seek truth and develop our capacity to give love. Our experience of *knowing* is deepening and expanding, moving beyond the limits of the rational mind to include the wisdom of the heart and the natural resources of the body. We are finding ourselves called to create purposeful lives, contributing in some way to the greater good.

As we look at our evolution from a developmental point of view, we can see how basic life understandings have changed as we have evolved: our sense of identity; sense of self; relationship with nature; our bodies, and our masculine and feminine aspects; as well as our concept of spirituality or connection with a higher power, life force or God.

Diagram 1:2 on the next page summarizes our evolution from Primal People to Conscious/Compassionate People.

Reconnecting With Nature: Reclaiming Our Wholeness

In our evolution as a species we are being forced to rediscover our own nature as well as the nature of life. In our separateness we have forgotten or denied essential pieces of ourselves,

DIAGRAM 1:2

OUR EVOLUTION FROM PRIMAL PEOPLE TO CONSCIOUS/COMPASSIONATE PEOPLE

	Where We Have Come From:	**Where We Have Been:**	**Where We Are Going:**
Our Developmental Stage	Primal people: newborn children. Nature is parent.	Thinking people: adolescents. God is parent.	Conscious/compassionate people: both parent and child.
Our Sense of Identity	Part of nature—something larger than self. Separate personal identity not yet defined.	Separate from nature and different than other people. Differentiation.	Part of nature while maintaining a unique sense of self. Reconnection, integration.
Our Relationship with Nature	Nature has power over humans. Nature in control.	Strive to have power over nature. Humans in control.	Co-creators with nature in our evolution. Creative power is part of our nature; the power of nature works through us.
Our Concept of God	Nature as creator and provider—an outside power—source of all which humans are vulnerable to.	God in our image—an outside power who judges, rationalizes, and determines what is "right."	God as a life force, a creative power residing inside and working through every human being.
Our Relationship With Our Bodies	At the mercy of the body. Mind is used to keep body alive.	Mind over matter. Body as subject of the mind.	Partnership of mind and body. Each a source of wisdom.
Prevailing Energy	Feminine energy predominates.	Masculine energy predominates.	Moving toward the balance of both energies.

have lost touch with the feminine and so have lost touch with our source of creative power. As a society we are connected to our producer, doer, the masculine side of our nature and are uncomfortable with the flow of life, the receptive, the feminine side. The Earth, the darkness, the heart and the flow of life are all feminine aspects.

Through our need to know or to control through knowing, we have become too action-oriented, too product-oriented; we have lost touch with the inner process from which action and products emerge. We are disconnected from the rhythms of life. We have raped the earth, run from the darkness, denied the heart and done our best to control everything from fear and lack of consciousness. Technology and mind knowledge are powerful tools, yet they are not sufficient to sustain life separate from nature.

To reclaim our full power as creative beings we must expand our way of thinking and living to consider both nature and technology, head and heart, the directive and the uncertain, dark and light. We need to recapture the sense of wonder we knew as a child and blend it with the passion, the sense of responsibility and the ability to act that we have learned as an adult. We are called to an integrated life.

Natural Principles for Conscious/Compassionate People

The fundamental principles and models we need to understand the life of nature, nature of life and to live fully as human beings in this next phase of evolution have been with us since the beginning of time. These organic principles include symbiosis, cooperation, wholeness, sustainability, interdependence, natural rhythm, balance and evolution. The current myth of separation obscures our interdependence and inherent wholeness. (See Diagram 1:3.)

A fundamental principle of nature is adaptability, the evolution of species in cooperation with the environment. The rigidity of the human mind has limited our adaptability, has led us to ignore nature and disconnected us from the creative, ongoing direction of life-sustaining forces.

DIAGRAM 1:3

NATURAL PRINCIPLES FOR CONSCIOUS/ COMPASSIONATE PEOPLE

Principle	What this means	Example from nature
Symbiosis	A group of individual parts working together in a complementary manner.	People breathe oxygen and release carbon dioxide. Plants breathe carbon dioxide and release oxygen.
Cooperation	Working *with* others rather than over, under, for or against them.	In a flock of birds one leads until tired, at which point a new lead bird takes over.
Wholeness	Each organism is a complete system including both male and female energies.	Flowers have both stamen and anthers.
Sustainability	The ability to live in the present to ensure the future of life.	Animals eat just the food they need.
Interdependence	All life forms are interrelated and need one another for their individual and collective survival.	The bee helps fertilize flowers as it collects pollen.
Natural Rhythm	The rhythm of life, including the life cycles, ebbs and flows.	The four seasons. The tide.
Balance	The cycles move toward a center, a steady place of peace.	A tree's branches sway in the breeze, coming to stillness when the breeze has passed.
Evolution	Change and growth toward a higher purpose.	The progression of all species: fish, mammals, people.

The models of nature are whole and complete. As we move from the world of thinking people to the world of conscious/compassionate people, rather than discount or reject old ways of living as inherently bad our frame of reference will expand to include more aspects of wholeness, from a static, two-dimensional perspective to a dynamic, three-dimensional one.

Knowledge of the Mind, Wisdom of the Heart

We have reached a point in our evolution where in order to truly "know" we must tap new resources. Underneath our need for answers is a deeper hunger for truth. The truth is something we can't be given but something we have to find and experience for ourselves. Our attempt to know in a logical, linear way has disconnected us from our own experience and, in essence, from the process of living. In this process, we've lost our ability to relate, to connect with others and often ourselves in a deep meaningful way. We have tried to control life through knowing rather than to engage and orchestrate life through experience.

We can always recognize truth by the way we feel inside. Feelings are a way to access our deeper truth. While at first this may surprise you, deep down you will know it is right as though there's a tugging in your gut that says, "Yes, that's so." Sooner or later knowing the truth brings you to a place of peace. Seeing things from a more relaxed place, you can breathe more comfortably and deeply.

While our heads are intelligent, our hearts are wise. The head knows through holding facts and information. The heart has a different kind of knowing—knowing through experience. Knowing leads to understanding that, in turn, leads to wisdom.[2] The heart is the caretaker of wisdom. In the heart we will find and recognize what is true. Our hearts know what really matters, what we want and what we care about. Through the heart we can make connections with self, with others and with life itself. To deny the heart is to deny truth.

In the rational world, the heart is given little credence. Our way of living and working discounts, invalidates or denies the heart. Your heart may tell you "reality" isn't workable. If you are invested in how things are, you might not want to know this. The heart's language is qualitative, hard to quantify, justify or even put into words. How do you explain what you care about to people who won't listen? How can you handle the tension between what you *know* to be true and the way things are? Can you trust your heart when you feel weak or vulnerable? Are the heart's concerns valid or even important? Society sees vulnerability as negative. Yet what we are talking about is seeing things from the heart's perspective. There's a difference between the vulnerability of being raw and wounded and the vulnerability that comes with an open heart. Our challenge is learning to orchestrate the openness and vulnerability of the heart.

Most of us are afraid to face the truth, to let ourselves know what we know and to act on that. Correspondingly, many of us are afraid to listen to our hearts. If facing the truth involves giving up a habit, a belief, a relationship, a job or a way of living, fear of the loss may keep us from following our hearts. One of my therapy clients, engaged in an affair that he hadn't told his wife about, one day admitted,

> If I were true to myself, I wouldn't be in either relationship. I really need to spend some time alone to get to know myself better. However, I lack the courage to do it. I'm afraid to be alone. I would hurt Mary and Edna if I separated from them. I don't want to feel their pain. I don't want to feel the pain within myself.

Until the price for ignoring the truth becomes greater than the price for facing it, my client will continue to run from what he knows to be true, ignoring the wisdom of his heart. Right now that seems to be safer. In facing the truth one allows the heart to open. Trapped in a marriage that was not meeting her needs, another client commented one day, "The truth may be painful, but not knowing the truth is even more painful." As she felt her pain, she opened her heart.

Living from the heart in a world that worships the rational, that separates head from heart, is painful and lonely. Yet to close off the heart, is to feel empty and incomplete. Nature values wholeness. In nature, there is a place for both head and heart.

Until you can learn to listen to your heart, you are operating with incomplete information. Closing your heart, you lose touch with your own nature and the natural world. You lose your sense of self, your sense of purpose and your sense of the sacred. Is it any wonder in our worlds of separation that we have almost destroyed our common home, our common provider, the Earth?

Living with Vision

As our species evolves, we are being asked to reassess our understanding of life and the way we live. Living with vision is a way of life for conscious/compassionate people who wish to create the future in partnership with nature.

Living with vision means viewing life as a process that is purposeful, constantly changing, and that clarifies each moment that we live and each step we take. It is a way of living as a complete, purposeful, compassionate and always human being, learning to tap and utilize our potential and creative power.

Living with vision requires us to rediscover our own nature, to recognize the part we play in the larger life drama, and to develop our ability:

- to see the way things are,
- to see how things can be,
- to know what needs to be done to get from where we are to where we are going,
- to know what part we are to play in partnership with others,
- to feel the inspiration and the impulse to act, and
- to take appropriate action.

Living with vision means recognizing that we have a unique role to play, a contribution to make, and that we make the contribution in being who we are as well as in doing what we do. This includes an understanding that caring brings conviction and conviction inspires action. Living from the heart does not breed weakness but strength and dignity.

Making a Difference

If "living with vision" encapsulates *how* we can live as conscious/compassionate people, "making a difference" is *why* it matters that we live this way. By nature, few of us can be truly content or fulfilled if we feel that our lives are wasteful or purposeless.

To be successful in today's society, one must jump through a series of hoops to achieve financial security, professional achievement and material well-being. *Doing it right* totally evades questions of meaning or purpose, of who one truly is deep down inside. Doing it right can bring social acceptance and creature comforts without addressing the more basic needs and desires: for peace, love, community and full self-expression. We don't want to go it alone in life, nor see our efforts go for naught. At some level I feel strongly that each of us has a sense of responsibility and a desire to positively impact the human condition and improve the quality of life on Earth.

Our desire to feel connected to others and the world, to contribute to society and know that something is better because we've been here, is what I call our desire to "make a difference." In past generations, many did this through raising children who became their legacy and contribution. Today, while for many children are still a legacy and contribution, we also want to take a stand, to find a place and to act on our convictions. As conscious/compassionate people we are called to work together to take responsibility for our lives and our future.

Service

Vision and love are closely related. Vision lives in the heart and is an expression of our love for self, others and the world. Living with vision is living from the heart, putting love into action. In this sense love is at the heart of service. Love travels in circles — when we give it we tend to get it, and when we get it, it's fun to share. Acting out of love is invigorating and fulfilling in and of itself. Love has a striking quality, and, while often hard to put into words, is unmistakable when you experience it.

Living from the heart creates a quality of service that touches others deeply and lastingly. The quality of service we give is often more important than the details of what we do. "Service is giving back to Life the gift of life—with interest."[3] Living with vision is creating a quality of life that nourishes and sustains the visionary and all others in our path. As we learn to live with vision, we find life to be fuller, more directed and truly abundant.

CHAPTER 2

The Nature
of Vision

Living with vision is walking the line of paradox—
there's loss, there's fullness, love and hate, joy
and sadness, exhilaration and fear.
Visionaries know this and are still able to walk
the line as they go forward—open to everything
that happens and responding accordingly.
—PHIL SARDELLA,
ORGANIZATION DEVELOPMENT CONSULTANT

Most simply stated, vision is our creative power. Vision is our ability as human beings to want, sense, imagine and bring into being new forms, structures and possibilities in partnership with life. Vision enables us to cooperate with life's higher purpose, reaching far beyond our own limits toward our highest and most passionate aspirations. When people ask me, "What do you mean by 'vision'?" I want to answer. While I know intimately what it feels like to live from vision, I am often tongue-tied when trying to put that feeling into words as though words cannot possibly express the depth of the experience. As one friend says, describing vision is "speaking the unspeakable." While best understood through personal experience, the essence of vision can be reflected in words.

A jewel with many facets, vision is by nature wholistic—it relates to our lives overall and to all the parts of our lives. We can have visions for ourselves, for others, for our communities, and for the world. Visions can be simple or outrageous, from wishing things were better to seeing beyond the realm of what appears possible. Vision reflects what we care about most, what really matters, what we hold sacred. The healthier we are, the more fully we can live with vision and make the unique contribution that is ours to make.

Why Does Vision Matter?

Vision is dismissed by many as idle fantasy, naive idealism or impractical thinking. Vision is neither idle nor fantasy, neither naive nor impractical, but is a very practical tool by which we create the blueprint for our desired future. Vision enables us to realize our hearts' desires, providing form and expression to our sense of purpose.

> ...Human nature is such that we are frequently prevented from seeing that what is taken for today's unorthodoxy is probably going to be tomorrow's convention. Perhaps we just have to accept that it is God's will that the unorthodox individual is doomed to years of frustration, ridicule and failure in order to act out his role in the scheme of things, until his day arrives and mankind is ready to receive his message: a message which he probably finds hard to explain, but which he knows comes from a far deeper source than conscious thought.
>
> —Charles, Prince of Wales[1]

Vision is the tool of conscious evolution. All of us can use this tool proficiently, applying it in all parts of our lives. Vision enables us to use our power to make a difference. It helps one understand both the larger scheme of things and where we fit in.

Vision provides a focus for our lives and a context out of which to make choices, invest time, money and personal energy, and view individual events. Vision is something to hold on to at those times when there's nothing to grasp, when daily life, job, relationships, home or sense of self are in transition.

Vision is the source of new models, images and structures for our lives and our world. As the old breaks down, vision creates the new. In the face of what isn't working we become clearer about how we want things to be. As we confront pressing problems we are moved to find alternative solutions. Vision enables a look at the possibilities.

Vision offers hope and possibility. When nothing makes sense we need something in which to have faith. Vision helps us imagine how things might be when we feel limited by how things seem to be. Vision asks us to have faith, to trust the way life works. Faith holds on to vision.

The Nature of Vision

> Would we humans knew our hearts in truth, nothing on earth would be impossible for us.
> —Paracelsus, 16th century healer

Over time I have developed a definition of what I understand vision to be:

Everyone has it...

...even though we often attribute vision to a few great leaders like Mahatma Gandhi, John F. Kennedy, and Martin Luther King. When comparing ourselves to these leaders, we feel small and conclude that they had abilities we couldn't possibly have. Each of these people played an important role in the world, and each drew upon their capacity for vision, but that capacity is not what makes them unique. We all have the capacity for vision and may simply not have learned to identify or use it.

Vision is a creative power.

Vision lives deep inside us. As we learn to use this power, we can draw upon our many natural resources. The creative impulse or spark starts in the heart, is fueled by passion, supported by will and managed by the conscious mind. As the fire burns within, we are inspired to act, to do what is needed to make vision real.

Translating an idea into a physical form, a painting, a manuscript or a machine is a step-by-step process.

Visions are desired realities.

Visions reflect how one really wants things to be and often differ from "the way things are," or current reality. In this sense, vision is the foundation on which everyone can build and create the new. The most mundane elements of our lives (like shopping malls, candy wrappers and paper towels) and the more elaborate ones (like the space program, great works of art and computer technology) all started with someone's vision. Visions are pre-realities. The gap between how things are and how one wants them to be provides the impetus, tension and momentum necessary for change.

> I say to you today, my friends, even though we face the difficulties of today and tomorrow, I still have a dream. It is a dream deeply rooted in the American dream. I have a dream that one day this nation will rise up and live out the true meaning of its creed, "We hold these truths to be self-evident that all men are created equal." I have a dream that one day on the red hills of Georgia sons of former slave owners will be able to sit down together at the table of brotherhood. I have a dream that one day even the state of Mississippi, a state sweltering with the heat of injustice, sweltering with the heat of oppression, will be transformed into an oasis of freedom and justice. I have a dream that my four little children will one day live in a nation where they will not be judged by the color of their skin, but by the content of their character.
>
> I have a dream today![2]
>
> —Martin Luther King

Visions are multi-sensory.

People can experience vision kinesthetically, sense it intuitively, see it as a visual image, hear it in words or sounds, or feel it deeply emotionally. Sometimes one has a sense of vision that can't be put into words. Whether it is experienced in sounds, sensations, images or feelings depends on one's natural style at that particular moment. When I write songs, first I hear a melody in my head, then I ground it by touching the piano keys with my fingers.

Visions are alive, just as we are.

Visions constantly grow and evolve. Each time a vision is revisited, some parts will be new and some parts familiar. Over time visions become clearer and are more deeply assimilated into our conscious minds and whole being. As this happens, the vision changes from a concept, idea, sense or feeling to a compelling force which emanates from the very center of one's being. In this sense, a vision is like the fruit of a fruit-bearing tree.

Visions are present-centered.

While vision directs us toward the future, it is experienced in the present moment. For the vision to become clear, real, and tangible may take time, however one can connect with an emerging vision at any moment. Look into your heart and ask what you really want or what really matters. In the moment and over time vision provides a focus for conscious attention. Vision helps attract and recognize opportunities and move away from situations that won't serve you.

Vision develops according to a natural timetable.

While one can define timeframes in which one would like to achieve a vision and consciously take actions that support your goals, ultimately you cannot control the time needed for a vision's realization. Trying too hard to control the natural timeframe of a vision can smother and extinguish the creative spark. A favorite saying of mine has always been, "Things of quality have no fear of time." When working in partnership with nature, one must honor and follow a larger timeclock than the one worn on the wrist or hung on the wall. There is a universal timeclock, a natural rhythm of life. You connect to this rhythm through your own heart, through your own heartbeat. As you learn to trust that natural rhythm, you learn when to act and when to wait.

> It would be very interesting to record photographically, not the stages of a painting, but its metamorphoses. One would see perhaps by what course a mind finds its way toward the crystallization of its dream. But what is really very serious is to see that the picture does not change basically, that the initial vision remains almost intact in spite of appearance.
> —Roger Sessions, American composer

Living with vision is the process of living as full, creative human beings.

Focusing on the immediate results we wish to achieve, we often forget that life is a process with many steps along the way. When you live with vision, you will attain many of your desired outcomes. However there is more to the process than achievement alone. Living with vision is a quality of life, one in which you get to know yourself very well, find time for self-care and balance reflection with action. You need to reach deep inside yourself to build a foundation for reaching far out into the world.

There are times when one looks for vision and finds "nothing" there.

When this happens we may conclude incorrectly that we did something wrong. Everything that has ever been created started with nothing. This is part of the process. Living with vision requires asking the little voice inside that judges our performance to suspend criticism long enough for us to accept whatever we see.

The four qualities that I have found essential in living with vision are:

1. authenticity—willingness to be truthful to whatever one sees to be true;
2. clarity—the ability to sense and articulate the vision fully;
3. purposefulness—a compelling sense of clearly directed motivation; and
4. commitment—the choice to own the vision, to embrace and do whatever is necessary to make it real.

All these qualities require courage and conscious choice.

> My vision is to have role models throughout the world for the traditional woman who is a mother, homemaker and wife... a model to represent that we can be whole, stand alone when necessary, but choose to pursue our desires, visions and creations with strength and dignity... not to have to accomplish our positions in submission or rebellion to men, society, and culture... for us to see representatives of womankind showing how they made it possible to achieve and take risks in spite of fear of abandonment or threatened loss of security. These special women would come forth to show us the many paths we may take in order to grow into our *own*—vision.
> —Marcia Gorfinkle, director of customer service

Language and Understanding: How We Talk About Vision

Language is an incredible mirror. Words both reflect the degree of our self-understanding and facilitate that understanding. When you understand something clearly you can usually find simple words to express it. There is a direct relationship between the clarity of my thoughts and the clarity of my language. For a long time I have reacted to the language people use when talking about vision. Phrases such as *taking control*, *setting goals*, *doing affirmations*, *visualizing what you want*, and *becoming the predominant creative force in our lives* triggers a little voice inside that says, "Something is missing. What?"

In the thinking stage of evolution, people have understood vision as a mental discipline: a carefully managed series of thoughts and actions. We have tried to reduce vision to a formula that says that if we program our minds with a series of words and images, and discipline ourselves to take a series of actions, we can manifest whatever we want. While the mind is a powerful tool and can indeed create anything we imagine, what matters is from where the impetus for creating comes. We often act out of fear rather than heartfelt desire. What we think we want may not really be so. What we create may not be what is needed and right for our life ultimately.

The Sure Thing or the Risk of the Unknown

John has been a management consultant, facilitating change in a large multi-national corporation, receiving considerable recognition, acknowledgement and financial reward. Just recently he resigned his secure position without knowing where he will work next.

> I'm tired and I've got a lot of thinking to do. I need some time. My former company keeps asking me to take on one project or another. It's tempting, and yet that's just what I'm trying to avoid. It's nice to be in demand, to be wanted. I could be very rich yet very lost. It's scary not knowing what will happen to me and where I'll go next. Somehow I need to find a way to give myself the space not to know. I know it's scary, yet it's what I need.

As thinking people we've focused our energy on being comfortable and feeling in control. To lessen our uncertainty and discomfort we have developed a wide variety of tools such as goal setting, affirmations and visualization. These tools enable us to define and hold a focus and consciously direct our energy, yet we often forget that tools which facilitate the creative process are not the process itself. We can become addicted to the tools, hoping they'll provide relief or answers. In our thinking stage we have confused using our creative power with being in control and making things happen. As we evolve we are reminded that the creative process involves constant change, learning when to hold on and when to let go, becoming familiar with uncertainty and learning to work with it rather than in spite of it.

Learning to Let Go

For much of my life I thought of myself as a person who could make things happen. I was a high-achiever. I looked very successful in the eyes of the world. I was a doer—a master of planning and control. I set and achieved goals through commitment and perseverance, managing every minute of my time with great skill and attention. While I felt great when people called me a dynamo, I didn't let myself stop long enough to realize how sad and weary I often felt.

Three years ago I was compelled to change the way I lived. While on the outside I seemed to have it all, inside something was missing. A voice inside of me said, "This isn't working. You're paying too big a price for your 'success.' You have to live differently." I knew the voice was right, yet I didn't know what to do. "What would it be like if I could 'let things happen,' instead of 'making things happen'?" I asked myself, and realized I didn't know how to *let* things happen. I felt that if I wasn't doing something, nothing would happen. The thought scared me. Being a dynamo was exhausting and didn't feel right. Yet it was the only way I knew to live, the only self-image I had.

I realized that while I knew how to generate and produce almost anything, I didn't know how to attract what I needed. I was a one-way battery, putting out continuously without ever getting recharged. With trepidation and courage I let go of my dynamo self-image and chose to learn how to attract as well as generate what I needed. At first I felt uncomfortable and uncertain, often powerless, and did not know what to do. My focus on achievement, action and planning had not left time or space for the unexpected.

As I learned to become comfortable with silence and reflection and to let go of having to act, I found myself moved to action in an entirely new way. I focused on what I really cared about. My desire to act became a natural impulse rather than a mandate of my mind. I acted out of inspiration and love rather than out of need and fear. I found myself expressing my heart as well as using my mind. I began to tap more of my passion than ever imagined and found myself coming to a deeper understanding about the nature of vision. In retrospect I realize it was a time of learning to love myself, to trust my instincts and my intuition, and to stop worrying about "doing it right." I was reclaiming my wholeness and my natural way of being.

As we evolve from the thinking to the conscious/compassionate stage in our development, we gain a fuller understanding of what vision is. As our understanding grows, the language used to describe vision needs to evolve as well. Diagram 2:1 on the next page illustrates how our framework for understanding vision expands. I will discuss how this changing framework affects the language we use to talk about vision.

Thinking Language

The language we've used as thinking people reflects our understanding of vision as a mental process focusing on achieving desired outcomes. To achieve these goals you draw on the power of the mind, create pictures and images that represent where you want to go and develop the mental discipline of reviewing them regularly, comparing your progress with your goals. The language is masculine and directive: *taking control*, *making things happen*, and *choosing*. Emphasis is placed on taking action, performance and achievement. The quality of the power you draw upon is masculine.

DIAGRAM 2:1

THINKING VIEW vs. CONSCIOUS/COMPASSION- ATE VIEW OF VISION AND LANGUAGE

DIMENSION	THINKING VIEW	WHAT'S MISSING	CONSCIOUS/ COMPAS- SIONATE
Aspects of Self	Masculine aspects	Feminine aspects	Wholistic—both masculine and feminine parts
Imagery	Linear	Circular	Spiral
How things are created	Achievement	Organicity	Conscious evolution
Where we focus our attention	Results	Process	Results understood in the context of process
Role of head and heart	Mental process	Heart-centered process	Collaboration of head (manager) and heart (source)
The nature of process	Active (doing)	Reflective (being)	A balance of reflection and action (being and doing)
Where we reach toward	Outward to the world	Inward to self	Inner depth provides foundation for reaching into the world
How we manage the process	Being in control (directive)	Being in harmony (relational)	Rationality in a context of uncertainty (directive and relational)

What's missing?

What's missing in the language we've developed are the feminine aspects of vision. While the masculine view of vision is directive, the feminine view of vision is relational, focusing on *how* things are achieved as well as *what* is achieved. The masculine perspective might ask, "What have you done?" The feminine perspective might ask, "How have you done it and how has this affected others?" Being in control is less valued than working in harmony with others and nature. Vision is a way of life that includes more than achieving desired results. The focus is on nurturing and cultivating yourself and your vision, letting actions emerge over time. The feminine view recognizes the heart as the source of vision. To connect with what you really want, you need to look into your heart.

A participant in a Money, Work and Personal Purpose workshop that I facilitated once told me, "Vision itself is a masculine word. *Finding one's voice* might be the feminine translation of *finding one's vision*." Having something to say and putting it out in the world may be the feminine expression of power.

> Living with vision is being able to present your soul in what you say, in the way you relate to people.
> —Rosemary LeBeau, photographer

Conscious/Compassionate language

Conscious/compassionate language includes both the masculine and feminine aspects of vision. Vision is by nature wholistic: a cycle of conception, development, expression and completion.

Our creative power is part of nature, not separate from it. The words *living with vision* acknowledge that vision is more than a mental process to achieve desired outcomes. Living with vision focuses on both process and results, viewing achievement in a larger context of growth and evolution.

As we become conscious/compassionate people, we recognize the place of both heart and mind in living with vision: vision comes from the heart and is translated into form and action by the mind. Nature has its own sense of timing and its own ultimately "right" outcomes. Your role as a human being is to know yourself, to master your own instrument—your body—and your unique role in life's drama.

Power is understood to be an inner capacity, a natural resource we have to direct and express rather than an external commodity to get or give. Responsibility and commitment replace *control* as a way of understanding our role in the creative process. We need to be clear, intentional and deliberate in our choices and actions without being overly willful. We learn to balance our personal desires with a respect for the natural course of events. Through making choices and acting on them we consciously direct our energy while remaining aware that we are part of a larger picture.

Conscious/compassionate people understand vision to be clarity of direction in a context of uncertainty.

CLARITY IN A CONTEXT OF UNCERTAINITY

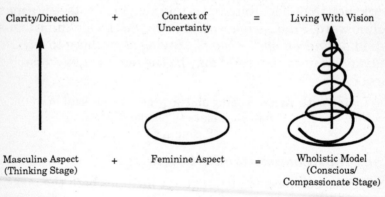

Clarity/Direction	+	Context of Uncertainty	=	Living With Vision
Masculine Aspect (Thinking Stage)	+	Feminine Aspect	=	Wholistic Model (Conscious/ Compassionate Stage)

DIAGRAM 2:2

Where Does Vision Come From?

When my heart fills with the spark of a new vision, a current of warm energy fills my entire body. I am reminded how being truly alive feels. Living with vision engages your entire body.

The *Heart* is where the impulse, the spark of vision, begins. Your *Passion* fuels the fire of vision, providing the support for growth, for sustenance. To grow and to thrive your vision needs conscious attention. You need to accept the vision, to choose it from a place deep inside, to sustain it and make it real. In this sense a vision, when you are truly committed to it, touches the *Soul*. You need to hold it sacred.

The *Mind* helps translate the impulse into action, identifying what needs to be done and how to do it. The *Will* exerts your power when needed and surrenders when you need to get out of the way to let the vision grow. With your *Voice* you express your vision, sharing it with others, putting it forth into the world. Your *Hands* enable you to do what needs to be done—taking those steps outlined by the mind.

> My vision: the land and other natural resources of this planet in a stable, sustainable balance with its inhabitants' needs and desires—a dynamic symbiosis.
>
> —Joan Hastings, co-director,
The Gaea Center for Art and Ecology

Vision and Creation: A Model from Nature

While writing this book, I have often felt pregnant. The book, starting as a seed deep inside me, has grown and evolved over time, becoming the tangible form you are now reading. The process through which a child develops serves as a natural model to understand how visions evolve and are realized. For simplicity, I've broken the process into five stages.

In actuality, spelling out the exact stages of a vision is hard—especially as things are happening. When you look back at the evolution of a vision, however, the stages can be seen clearly. The story of Good Company, a music production cooperative, illustrates how a vision and the organization it has brought into being have evolved over time.

Stage 1: Conception

The seeds of Good Company were sown in 1978 when two of the founding members—Dennis Pearne, 37, and Marian Streetpeople, 30—were driving home to Boston late at night from a gig in Carabassett Valley, Maine. Both were members of a seven-piece rock band committed to doing original music wherever they played. "The music scene was brutally competitive and as we talked about that something very obvious occurred to us: that ultimately cooperation, not competition, is the appropriate mode for artists to function in. That idea stayed with us and eventually we had a chance to put it into practice," recounts Dennis.[3]

Stage 2: Differentiation

Dennis and Marian went their separate ways in 1981. Each of them put together bands and continued playing in the Boston music scene. In 1983 Dennis was part of a topical folk quartet, Rising Tide, that decided to produce an album and release it on their own label. "We were going to call the band either Rising Tide or Good Company," recalls band member Barbara Herson, 40. "We called the band Rising Tide, and Good Company became our production company." Dennis had also been hired to engineer the album of two other musicians, Bette Phelan and Peggy Morgan, who had their own label for recording and publishing their songs.

In the process of recording the album came the idea of releasing the album under the Good Company label. Suddenly, Good Company had two albums to its credit.

Collaboration and cooperation were already evident in the relationship between Good Company musicians. Dennis had bartered his engineering skills in exchange for Bette's illustration skills. She drew the cover for the Rising Tide album in exchange for Dennis' engineering time.

Stage 3: Growth to Clarity/Functionality

While the albums were being produced on the business end, Rising Tide's members, Marian, and several other musicians began to gather weekly to play music, sing and talk as friends. Everyone lived within five minutes of one another so getting together was easy to do. Barbara's kitchen became the womb in which the production company grew and developed, while its members were nourished by Barbara's cooking. The gatherings provided an incubator for self-discovery as the friends explored who they were and what mattered to them. In time, a sense of group identity evolved. The group became a community—a family of friends, with many kinds of relationships between group members: music, business, love and friendship. As a choice was made for Good Company to be a formal production company, most members chose to be part of it, and one member did not. In 1984, Good Company produced two more albums, and organized its first annual company concert.

DIAGRAM 2:3

STAGES IN THE DEVELOPMENT OF A VISION

Characteristics	Common reactions
STAGE 1: CONCEPTION	
Vision may not be perceptible	Nothing is there
Occurs deep inside of us	I need to see it or feel it to
Reflects a conscious choice to be open to the creative process	believe something is there
STAGE 2: DIFFERENTIATION	
Some elements of the vision begin to identify themselves	There's something going on, but I don't understand it.
The visionary can begin to identify parts of the vision	Can I trust what I sense?
STAGE 3: GROWTH TO CLARITY/FUNCTIONALITY	
All the major parts of the vision are clear conceptually	Now that I have a clear picture of what to do, what do I do about it?
A course of action can be determined to begin making the vision real	What do I do about the things I don't know or don't have?
	Am I willing to invest my time, money and energy in making this thing real?
STAGE 4: BIRTH	
A commitment has been made to make the vision real	Now that I'm committed, can I trust the process?
A clear purpose, course of action, and a plan have been developed	What will other people think of me as I go about this effort?
The vision moves from the womb of the creator into the world at large	
STAGE 5: LIFE/IMPLEMENTATION	
The visionary continues along a course of action, meeting obstacles and successes	How long will this take? Will the process ever end?
The visionary is forced to re-examine goals, commitment, clarity and course of action	Can I stand it any longer?
The visionary feels purposeful, focusing on the expression of the vision in the world	Am I crazy to be doing this?
The visionary is stretched personally in living the vision— give up, the vision dies—keep going, and the vision is realized in its own time	I feel compelled to do this, to follow my heart.

Stage 4: Birth

The first Good Company concert was a coming-out party featuring over half a dozen performers. "We are a group, this is our music and we want you to know about it," were the sentiments behind the event. The company learned a lot about production in organizing the concert. "We discovered that some people wanted to do the organizing and some people saw themselves only as performers," recounts Barbara. In this discovery the group faced a new question: How could they define each member's contribution and balance what got put in and what got taken out of the company? Collectively they generated lots of publicity, including articles in the two major Boston newspapers, attracting 150 people to the concert. "During the concert we really listened to one another's music—to the lyrics and not just the technical parts. We created the company through the music that night," remembers Marian. "There was a feeling of joining together to project something you believe." A great success, the event also unearthed problems and challenges that the group would have to face as it continued to evolve: promoting the group versus promoting the individual, the relationship between the individuals and the group, and the question, "How successful will we be?"

Stage 4: Life/Implementation

At a weekend retreat in 1987 the collective expanded their boundaries to include poetry, sculpture and photography as well as music. Today, Good Company includes 11 artists and features five albums and a variety of other creations including poetry books and tapes. "We enjoy one another's work, have an interest in each other's lives, and have a history together," related Marian. The group recently produced its fifth annual Good Company concert. Some sub-groupings within the company have changed over the years—Barbara and Marian are now music partners, Dennis leads a band with two newer members—while others have endured—Bette and Peg are still a duo as are two other members, Chris and Daya Doolin.

The individual artists have grown stronger and more successful in their own right. Barbara has her own company, Earthtunes, offering environmental-education music programs for children. Bette and Peg tour often, their travels taking them as far as Australia. Members live in different towns, several in different states. The core of the group currently meets once a month to share information about gigs and work on song-writing assignments; they also share promotional expenses and a post office box.

"In the future I see us meeting less often, because it will be harder for us to get together," shared Marian. "Everyone is growing stronger in their own right. Everyone has their own direction." Looking at the group's evolution in retrospect, Barbara recognizes, "It allowed me to have the vision and strength to do my own children's program." "Perhaps the purpose of the group has been to provide musical and emotional nutrients to support our growth process," reflects Marian. Only time will tell how the group is to evolve. However, Marian, Dennis and friends have come a long way from their roots in living their vision.

What Vision Is and What Vision Is Not

We often confuse vision with other tools and inner resources including visualization, intuition, images, beliefs and fantasies. While these tools and resources may be part of living with vision, vision is more than any one of these alone. The following chart (Diagram 2:4) explores the place of each of these tools and resources in living with vision.

DIAGRAM 2:4

RESOURCES OFTEN CONFUSED WITH VISION

VISUALIZATION	A powerful tool that draws on the mind's ability to develop pictures of what it wants to create—a projection of the mind, a clear, tangible picture that incorporates the details of what you want to create as seen in the mind's eye.
Its strengths:	Helps you remember, clarify and keep your energy focused on what you want.
Its limitations:	Without including the heart, you may create something you later discover isn't what you really wanted, or isn't right. The mind can create without a conscience.

DIAGRAM 2:4 CONT'D RESOURCES OFTEN CONFUSED WITH VISION

INTUITION	The part of you that recognizes what is true and real before you have the facts to justify what you know. Can be experienced as "gut feel," psychic insight or a deep sense of knowing.
Its strengths:	I've never gone astray when I've followed my intuition. It helps you know what's right for you, and stay on course particularly when your brain is confused or you don't know what to do.
Its limitations:	You may find it hard to trust your intuition. It isn't solid and concrete like facts and figures; it may be scary.

IMAGES	A symbol or representation of a vision, desire or aspiration. It may convey meaning beyond words, providing a tangible symbol of something intangible.
Its strengths:	Images provide something to hold on to or work toward creating as you journey through the unknown. They provide security.
Its limitations:	We forget that images are just symbols. Images from the world around you may not relate to what you care about or what is right for you, e.g., messages about doing it right, looking good, and being successful. You need to notice where images come from.

BELIEFS	Mental constructs, the programs we hold in our minds that structure our perceptions and our experience. Beliefs tell us what to expect, what not to expect, what behavior is consistent with who we think we are, and our concept of how life works.
Its strengths:	Beliefs provide certainty in a world of uncertainty. They enable us to respond consistently and habitually without even thinking. Since our beliefs create our reality, healthy beliefs enhance our quality of life.
Its limitations:	Beliefs may limit our ability to experience life moment to moment, and may interfere with our ability to see or respond genuinely to new or different situations. Beliefs grounded in painful experiences, particularly from childhood, may prevent us from creating what we really need—e.g., a woman abandoned as a small child may not know how to be supported by others and have a hard time believing she can count on anyone to be there when she needs them.

FANTASY	According to Webster's dictionary, "the power or process of creating unrealistic or improbable mental images in response to a psychological need."
Its strengths:	Fantasy is an attempt to find a way to meet an unfulfilled need. In this sense, it helps us take care of ourselves. Fantasies can be fun.
Its limitations:	Fantasy may not directly confront the need and say "What can I do about meeting the need in practical terms?" In this sense, fantasy can be a diversion or escape from practical reality.

Vision and Reality: Vision and Action

Our thinking world places a high value on action and on being *realistic*. Today we may err on the side of being too action-oriented, feeling a need to be doing something all the time for fear that if we stop nothing will happen. Reality is subjective, and one can easily lose a sense of self when faced with the limits and constraints of the world at large.

Some of us have a myth that vision is contrary to reality. Underneath this myth is a distrust of the heart and of passion and desire, a fear of our own nature, and a need to control in order to reduce our fear of the unknown. As you learn to trust your heart—paying more attention to what you value and care about, seeing more clearly what you need and what you actually have—the relationship between vision and reality will become clear.

Throughout human history, the individuals we recognize as great leaders had both vision and ability to act. In fact, vision usually *compels* us to act.

Norman Cousins, discussing what brought him to his work at the University of California, Los Angeles, stated:

> I came here with a driving obsession. It was a driving obsession to find the evidence, or to produce it, that the negative emotions were not the only ones that made their registrations in humans.
>
> Research had been done on the penalties produced by fear, rage, panic, exasperation and frustration, depression and the like. No comparable research had been done on the positive emotions: love, hope, faith, will-to-live, festivity, determination and so forth.
>
> And it didn't seem reasonable to me to believe that the body works only one way. Or that the only time the emotions make their registration is when the emotions are negative.
>
> So for the past ten years I have immersed myself in work and thought dealing with this aspect of human life. And now at the end of ten years I think we do have very substantial evidence, scientifically verifiable, that *all* emotions, not just the negative ones, have biochemical effects.
>
> And we've been able to show, in several research projects, that just as depression impairs the immune system, so being able to free patients from depression will enhance the immune system.[4]

CHAPTER 3

Discovering Your Purpose

Some time in our life we're called to climb
Called to become life's mountaineers.
Deep down inside a flame ignites
Lighting the way from inside...
—FROM "LIFE'S MOUNTAINEERS"

At the heart of living with vision is purpose. Purpose is what compels us to take a stand, to act with such conviction that we may surprise ourselves, and ultimately, it is what fulfills us. We live from purpose at times without even knowing it. Without purpose life is at best incomplete, at worst futile. Our sense of purpose is what connects us to ourselves and to all of life.

Purpose is not only at the root of a high quality of life, but also at the root of health. Hans Selye, a pioneer physician in the field of stress said, "It is a biological law that... man has to fight and work for some goal he considers worthwhile."[1] Negative stress is associated with feelings of uselessness, worthlessness and futility. If you spend your time doing things that aren't important or don't fully utilize your skills and talents, health and morale decline. Illness provides an invitation, sometimes a harsh one, to look at how you're living your life and to reassess what really matters. Likewise, when your motivation at work declines you may find that your work feels purposeless.

Over the last few years I have encountered more and more people searching for a sense of personal purpose. Many who have "made it," who have become successful by society's standards, still feel something is lacking. Others, having gone along the accepted path to a certain point, have lost the drive to go further. Still others become hopeless when faced with the harsh realities of our world today—war, illness, depletion of the Earth's natural resources, isolation, addiction and a spiritual hunger that goes unfulfilled.

"What's the point of it all?" "Why am I here?" "Is there not more to life than daily routine?" "Who am I really and where do I fit into all of this?" Inner voices that ask these questions grow louder and more compelling. Sooner or later we are called forth to embark on an inner and outer journey that will last for the rest of our lives.

Surrender and Choice

Damon Reed, 48, left her successful career in the publishing industry several years ago to embark on a path of discovery and a way of living that is truer to the person she is.

> For most of my life I defined myself (as did others) as "the doer," "the achiever." When I left the corporate world, I gave myself permission not to *do* and began to distinguish between doing and just being who I am. After numerous titles and functions, with no definition of self, I was empty.
>
> The decision to leave my work of 13 years forced me to commit to an ongoing journey. It was both difficult and wonderful. The journey is about being very clear who I am and about being true to myself. I think this is at the root of most people's journeys. Different experiences and crises propel us toward clarity and journeys at different times in our lives.
>
> Much of my journey has involved letting go of my parents' mirrors—their oughts, their dreams, their expectations, their standards—and becoming comfortable and familiar with my own dreams, values, capabilities, and choices. Not until people are comfortable with themselves can they let go of or simply be with their parents' mirrors.
>
> To be on a personal journey to me means to seek one's vision, one's purpose in life, why one is here. Vision and

purpose don't come from our minds. They come from the silence within—from the depths of the soul. Purpose becomes a question that will not go away.

To be on the journey is to surrender to what might be. One needs to be open to life, to coincidences, to how things just show up, to choices we make in life, to the intriguing patterns inside ourselves and in life. My biggest challenges are when I'm in turmoil, when I'm upset. I ask the question, "Why am I doing this?" I'm such a head person it's been difficult for me to listen, to trust, and to follow my heart. When I have, I've felt joyful, open, and vulnerable in a gentle way—a vulnerability without fear, vulnerability accompanied by trust. Surrender is about trust beyond trust, about that unconditional giving over to life.

It requires courage to leave a familiar world to explore a new one. Damon had worked to build a solid identity in the world's eyes, then gave it up for something unknown, intangible, unfamiliar. And yet in choosing to be true to herself, to live fully and to be the person she really is, Damon has begun to live with purpose.

What Is Personal Purpose?

A running joke in our workshops has become, "How much does it cost to buy a purpose? Where can I get one?" We tend to treat purpose as a thing or object—something you are lacking and get rather than something you already have and rediscover. You may have been more aware of a sense of purpose as a child, keenly aware of what you loved, what mattered, and what moved you to act. As you grew older you were taught that the things that mattered to you didn't really matter. Money, career, looking good and doing it right became more important than enjoying the feeling of sunshine on your face as you sat in a field or wondering about the future of the Earth as real estate developers took over the field.

Somehow purpose changed from a sense of passion, attraction and aliveness to an intellectual construct quite confusing to the mind. I hope to demystify personal purpose and, through words and exercises, to create a mirror in which you can rediscover what you already know.

Purpose is your natural way of being in the world.

When you follow your heart, do the things that really matter to you, and respond instinctively to what you see and feel, you are living from your personal purpose.

Purpose asks you to be true to yourself.

As you live your life and explore what is meaningful, you discover what being true to yourself is all about.

Purpose asks you to return to your true nature.

Recognize the qualities and talents that are most naturally yours.

Purpose reminds you that life is a journey, a process.

Your understanding of who you are and what you will become is constantly unfolding.

Purpose gives you an anchor and a sense of direction.

As the world changes around you, purpose provides a sense of constancy and continuity. When something feels right you can say your course is "on purpose."

Purpose encourages you to adopt an attitude of service, asking yourself, "How can I help?"

In our hearts most of us want to make a difference, to contribute in some way to the greater good. Acknowledge that you are part of something larger than yourself, that all is interdependent and interconnected.

Purpose enables you to create ways of living and working that are fulfilling and sustainable.

Purpose becomes a screen through which to filter your activities and choices and a foundation on which to build your future.

Comments on Personal Purpose

I've been good with my hands all of my life. Things would come to me naturally. I thought everyone could do them but many could not. It takes patience to make something. I want to instill in people a quality of vision that enables them to distinguish between mediocre and really fine things. I can do a lot that people want and that's a service. What's unbelievable is that I'm doing what I want to do,... and I didn't even know I could get paid for it.

—Bill LeBeau, painter

It's great to be on fire— to not have enough hours in a day to do what I want to do. In my photography, I try to wait for the perfect moment when I see someone's soul through their eyes. In the work I do for myself I try to capture what's really important to me—family: my husband and my daughter.

—Rosemary LeBeau, photographer and mother

I believe in people, in the simpler aspects of human life, in the relation of man to nature. I believe man must be free both in spirit and in society, that he must build strength into himself, affirming the enormous beauty of the world and acquiring the confidence to see and to express his vision. And I believe in photography as one means of expressing this affirmation and of achieving an ultimate happiness and faith.

—from *Ansel Adams: An Autobiography*

I have a sense of an evolutionary direction in the universe. I feel best when I'm hooked up to it. As a human being, there are some givens, some good things. These include love, community, and a sense of getting as close as you can to transcendence. The work I've done over the years ties in with that evolutionary direction, be it films, dancing, community development, Co-op America or being a good parent or friend. I've learned a lot over the years. I tend to trust my own intuitions of what's good to do at any point.

—Paul Freundlich, founder and director, Co-op America

I feel strongly that the call for purpose is part of our evolution to adulthood as a species. In our adolescence we focused our attention on ourselves and didn't give a lot of thought to the world around us. As conscious/compassionate people, we are being forced to extend our vision beyond our personal lives and to take responsibility for our relationship with other living creatures and the world around us.

Purpose is at the root of being conscious/compassionate people. While we have always known that our minds, our ability to think, differentiated us from other living beings, we also have the power to create and destroy life like no other species can. At this phase in our evolution, with the future of life on Earth at stake, I feel we are being asked to cooperate with the evolutionary direction—call it life, God or nature. Purpose helps us define what we can do individually and collectively in order to collaborate, to work in partnership with the larger creative impulse that is life.

Your purpose can be expressed in many forms. This is where vision comes into the picture. Vision allows you to build a bridge between your sense of mission or personal purpose and the world you live in. Vision translates your sense of purpose into what it is you want to create and what you must do to create it. If vision is the what, purpose is the why. Together they help you discover how. How can you be the best person you can be? Do you want to create a friendship, an organization, a family? How will your actions impact those around you? How do you respond to what needs to be done? Purpose taps your natural power, vitality and creativity, and it moves you to act.

In a sense purpose provides a road map for your entire life. Vision provides a road map for different phases in your life. Large visions (like those of Martin Luther King, Buckminster Fuller, and Mahatma Gandhi) take a lifetime or more to be realized. Many of us complete one vision and move on to pursue a new vision. While the work you do may be very different, you can usually see how it relates at a fundamental level to the work you have just completed. Purpose is a common thread running through all you create and achieve over the course of your life.

Finding Your Personal Purpose

We live our lives out of certain truths. If you look at who you have been and what you have done you will discover threads running through your life representing consistent and essential patterns or themes. We each have a song that we sing throughout our lives everywhere we go in all we do. We sing the song in different ways at different times; yet, in essence, the song is the same. Just because you don't always remember the tune doesn't mean it isn't there or that you can't sing it. The search for personal purpose is to become familiar with your own voice, and what you express when you sing. The search begins inside of you.

Clues to Unearthing Your Purpose: The Inner Child

Children are much clearer about who they are and what really matters to them than adults. Somehow as we "grow up" in society we learn to build masks and layers over that basic knowledge. This knowledge, this sense of self, may become buried but it is still there. All of us have a child inside, a part that has not forgotten what has always been important to us, what has always been true. Inside the child is a flame which, when nurtured, can light the way. So often the sense of self is tramped down or extinguished when children are discounted, denied, not heard, or made to feel invisible. As an adult, you can begin to rediscover your inner child.

The following meditation will help you connect with that inner child and with your sense of purpose.[2]

Exploring Your Personal Purpose

Preparation

Get into a comfortable position. Close your eyes and take a deep breath. Give yourself all the time and space you need to breathe. And whenever you feel ready, take a moment to listen to your heart. See if you can feel it beating in your chest. Take a moment to become familiar with your heart, feel your pulse beating in your heart, in your arms, in your hands. Take a moment to find your pulse, your own natural rhythm.

Exercise

Allow yourself to locate the the child who still lives inside of you. Ask the child within to join with the adult you are today and answer the following questions:

What have you always loved?

What have you always known, even before you knew anything?

What has always felt true?

What has always come naturally to you?

What have you always cared about?

What parts of yourself do you keep coming back to again and again over the years?

Take as much time as you need to sit with these questions. When you are ready, ask your inner child to create an image which symbolizes your sense of purpose, why you are here, the truest, most basic, essential part of you.

When finished, very slowly and gently, at your own pace, take a deep breath and bring your focus back into the room. When you open your eyes, draw a picture that represents your sense of purpose, title it, and make some notes about your answers to the questions you have just explored.

Some tips about this exercise:

If you didn't come up with an image during the meditation don't be discouraged. See if you can make one up as you start recording your thoughts.

Draw a picture of the image with crayons, felt tipped pens or paint. This is a way to continue the process after you open your eyes. See if a picture emerges as you put pen or crayon to paper. Colors as well as words and symbols express your experience.

Record your questions and frustrations as well as your insights. All are part of the process.

This meditation can be done periodically. Reflecting on these questions over time invites new insights and memories to emerge.

Understanding Our Values: What Are They Really?

While the concept of values has been around for a long time, understanding what values are seems elusive. You can talk about them intellectually, engage in philosophical discussions, and yet struggle as you try to unearth them in your own life.

Methods for discovering and applying personal values often come up short because we look to the world around us rather than to our hearts for meaning. Most simply, values are what really matter to us, what is most important and essential. They help us understand our sense of purpose and enable us to feel connected to ourselves. Values clarify who you are and what you stand for. Your words and actions reflect your values.

Values are what you find at your core. While on the surface we may think money, position, and achievement are most important, what does matter to most of us are fairly basic things. Values can be unearthed by examining past actions and experiences, seeing what you loved and hated, what really mattered. In our workshops, Wynne Miller and I have found what people really value are

- Feeling connected, not alone
- Freedom
- Belonging (here on this Earth)
- Feeling loved and appreciated
- Feeling worthwhile and useful
- Feeling safe (that the environment is protective)
- Feeling seen or recognized or making a difference
- Being true to oneself and expressing one's truth
- Having one's personal uniqueness respected
- Feeling good about oneself
- Feeling whole and complete
- Having a strong sense of personal identity.

These core values reflect what we need to realize our potential as human beings.

The Place of Values in Living with Vision

Both our purpose and our values live deep inside us. Each provides a kind of root or anchor as we journey into the unknown. Values, like vision, live in the heart and reflect what matters most to us. Values can be unearthed by uncovering the themes and patterns that run through our lives, while vision is a projection of these themes and patterns into the future. The image of the tree helps illustrate the relationship. Vision is like the branches of a tree, reaching into the sky, the unknown. Like branches, vision is the growing edge of the tree, what we are becoming or are yet to become. Values are the roots of the tree, reaching down deep into the Earth, our source, connecting who we are now with who we have been. Roots provide the tree with nourishment as it grows and keep its footing in the face of winds, rain or other turmoil in the environment. In this sense, values provide a solid foundation for living with vision. The trunk of the tree can represent purpose, which is at your very center. To be balanced, you need to be connected to your purpose, your center, letting your values provide a foundation and your vision provide a direction for your actions.

Like the tree, as we grow we feel a tension in our trunk, in our center, as our branches pull us upward and our roots keep us steady. This creative tension grounds us and supports our ventures into the unknown. Robert Fritz' concept of structural tension[3] is similar to the pull I'm describing in the tree. Structural tension is the tension between where we are and where we want to be. Because tension seeks resolution, it provides momentum to help you get to where you want to be. If you let go of structural tension, you give up what you want to create or lose perspective on where you are. Recognizing that this kind of tension is structural and not emotional can help you learn to use it to your advantage.

Victor Frankl addresses this issue beautifully in *Man's Search for Meaning*.

> What man actually needs is not a tensionless state but rather the striving and struggling for a worthwhile goal, a freely chosen task. What he needs is not the discharge of tension at any cost but the call of a potential meaning waiting to be fulfilled by him.

Getting to the Root of the Matter

Exercise

This exercise is designed to unearth what is at your core, to discover your values by probing what really matters.[4] You can do it alone, but it is best done with a partner. Because the exercise examines what you loved and hated about the jobs you have had, it clarifies what you need for your work to be an expression of your purpose.

Step 1: Choose a work situation you would like to explore. You can include your current job as well as any past jobs. Both paid and unpaid work count. Projects and programs count; so does being a parent. Write the name of the job, the time period you had it and the organization you are/were part of at the top of a piece of paper.

Step 2: Choose three things you love about the job, and three things you don't like about the job. Write each of these down on the piece of paper as indicated in Diagram 3:1.

DIAGRAM 3:1

Name of Job: Clinical Psychologist
Time Period I Had Job: 1978-1981
Organization: St. John's Hospital

Three Things I Loved	*Three Things I Didn't Love*
1. Helping people	1. The politics
2. Working with children	2. The number of
3. My colleagues	clients I had to see
	3. The pay

Step 3: The basic procedure you're now going to use is the same whether you are working alone or with a partner. Choose one of the items you love or one of the items you didn't like that you want to probe. If you are working with a partner, give him your piece of paper so he can ask the questions and record your answers. If you are working alone, you will record your own answers.

Ask yourself what you love (or hate) about the particular thing you have chosen to work with. Write down the first answer or thought that comes to you. Then ask yourself, "And what do I love (or hate) about that?" Again write down the first answer or thought that comes to mind. Continue to ask yourself what you love about that until you feel you've gotten to the root of the matter. When you feel you're at the root, write down what is essential, what really matters.

Some tips for doing Step 3 : If you find yourself stuck, try different questions—"How did it feel?" or "If there were a voice inside you, what would it say?"

Here's what a sample dialogue might look like, using the person in Diagram 3:1...

Q. What didn't you like about the politics?

A. I felt the people were dishonest.

Q. And what didn't you like about that?

A. I couldn't trust them.

Q. And what didn't you like about that?

A. I felt uncomfortable.

Q. And what didn't you like about feeling uncomfortable?

A. I wanted to hide.

Q. And as you wanted to hide, if there were a little voice inside you, what would it have said?

A. I'm not safe here.

Q. And what didn't you like about feeling unsafe.

A. I need to feel safe. I couldn't be myself.

Q. Is safety a root for you?

A. I guess so. And being free to be myself.

Q. So how would you summarize what's at the root?

A. I need to be safe and I need to be free to be myself.

Step 4: Continue to go through the process outlined in Step 3 until you have unearthed the roots of all three items you loved and all three items you didn't love. You may want to try the exercise for several more work situations.

Step 5: Look at the roots you have dug up and ask the following questions:

Have any patterns emerged? For example, you may find the same core value emerging from something you loved as well as from something you hated.

What really matters to you? Make a list of the roots. (If you are working with a partner, have your partner add to the list based on his observations.)

Step 6: Read the list of roots over to yourself. Let your heart as well as your head see the list. Ask yourself the question, "What's at the core?" See if you can refine the list of roots/what matters down to a couple of key items. Ask yourself, "What's the essence here?"

Linking Your Purpose and Your Values

Your list of core values can help you live purposefully, even if the concept of purpose feels elusive. Reviewing the list can help you remember what matters, prioritize what needs to be done, and identify the support and resources you need. The things that matter apply to all parts of your life and all your activities. They can help you define the environment you want to live in, the work you want to do, and the people you want to be with. When built on what matters, your life can really work. If something doesn't work, you may have forgotten a core value.

Doing What Really Matters

Rich Esper, at 24, is a a person who lives true to himself and with vision. In the summer of 1986 he opened his own shop, the Village Cobbler in Shrewsbury, Massachusetts a vision he had been pursuing since childhood.

> I was 13 when I went to the Cobbler Shop in Westboro. The guy was looking for help. It was my first job. I started at $1.50 an hour. Right off the bat, I enjoyed it. The guy was great. He knew how to work and how to have fun. We had a lot of common interests and got along well together.
>
> I always liked doing things with my hands. I was never much for school, but I liked woodworking and metal shop in high school. As I learned to work on the machines in the cobbler shop, I found I liked them too. I also liked the feeling of fixing something for someone and having them be pleased. It felt good.
>
> My parents weren't thrilled that I was so much into shop work. They felt I should get an education—that I should be doing my homework. After high school I went to college. I chose a program that had work-study so I could work as well as be in school but I felt like a number there. I hated the city.
>
> After a couple of years, I quit college. I had missed the work I did as a cobbler. This kind of work means something to me. School didn't mean anything .
>
> I've had my own shop for a year and a half. I didn't think I was going to do it so quickly. I love my work. I tell people I'm a cobbler. I fix shoes, and I'm proud of it. There aren't too many people fixing shoes. I'm a craftsman. I'm trying to please people and do the best I can with my work.
>
> My parents weren't happy at first but now they're thrilled. You've got to take chances. You won't get anywhere if you don't. This is not a job. A job is a task— something someone does that they don't like. You've got to be happy. Work is for the rest of your life.

Personal Purpose and Meaningful Work

What is work? In our society work is often defined as a job or an occupation—something you do, a role you play. We often think of it as a burden, a necessary evil, something separate from *real life*. We usually don't bring our whole selves to work but instead put on a professional identity mask. This experience often stifles the human spirit and limits our ability to live true to ourselves. Work becomes empty and purposeless.

In living with vision the experience of work is not separate from *life* but is central to it. Work is the way you express your personal purpose in the world. Work becomes the series of steps you take to move toward your vision. In this sense, work is both purposeful and meaningful. Work is what you do because you want to do it, because you love it, and because you feel compelled to. The work setting is one place in which you create and express your vision—where you make a difference.

The trochus shell illustrates the place of meaningful work in living with vision. In Diagram 3:2, the shell is divided into three sections.

1. The top section represents your lifework, the culmination of all you give to the world over the course of your life through the way you live and the actions you take.

UNDERSTANDING MEANINGFUL WORK

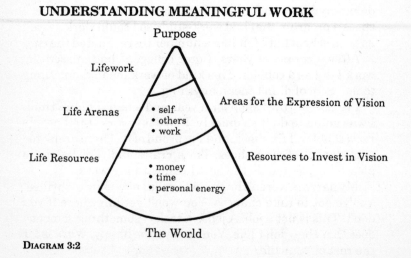

DIAGRAM 3:2

2. The middle chamber represents your life arenas—the places where you express yourself and give your gifts to the world. There are three fundamental arenas: self, others, and work. In the world as we know it, cultivating ourselves and our relationships is often not valued as highly as doing or producing through work. Yet you make a difference in being who you are as well as in acting in the world. All three arenas are places for growth, learning, and creative expression.

3. The bottom chamber represents your life resources, the materials available to invest in your work and all parts of your life. The three basic resources you have to manage as an individual are: money, time, and personal energy. All three resources need to be invested to support a vision and make it real.

Contributing to the Greater Good

At the heart of meaningful work is the contribution one makes to the greater good. While self-expression and personal gratification are part of meaningful work, both are limited when done in isolation. We are part of society and affected by it no matter how hard we try to ignore this or build a nest of security to protect us from our surroundings. Each of us can be agents to create a better world.

Many of us shirk at the thought of being a change agent. Perhaps the task seems too big. "What can I do?" you may ask. Perhaps the thought is too scary. Ironically, making a difference, being an agent of change, is a simple and natural process. You make the biggest difference by being the person you truly are and by showing up wherever you do as you go about your daily routine.

The places that naturally attract you are the places you are most likely to impact. For example, I take dance classes at the YWCA several days a week and have been doing so for several years. Today, on a creative whim, I brought a song to the dance class that I thought would be fun to move to. Because the teacher has become a friend of mine, she welcomed the song. As we warmed up our bodies, twelve people were listening to music they had never heard before. Most of them liked it. I felt really good. I had just made a difference.

Likewise, the issues we tend to impact are the ones we care about. There's a lot of work to be done in the world, and we need not waste energy chastizing ourselves for not taking action on those issues that are important in the larger scheme of things yet peripheral to us personally.

While I feel that the issue of toxic waste is important, I do not feel nearly so drawn to it as to issues of physical health and well-being. I am committed to helping individual people live more healthfully. While being mindful of all that needs to be done, if we each follow our convictions and do what we can, I believe that collectively all the world's major issues will be addressed positively.

Finding Meaningful Work

To develop a picture of what meaningful work would be for you, try the following:

Look at the things you love and have always loved. Build your work and your life around what you really care about.

Take a creative stance in choosing your work. Don't be limited by what you think is possible. Clarify how you'd like your work to be, and then find a way to do it. Looking for a *job* is very different than creating your work.

Give yourself permission for work to be fun and meaningful. Work does not have to be drudgery.

Think about the environment you'd like to work in, including the location, the physical surroundings and the number and kinds of people you'd like to work with.

Be courageous. Take risks. Living with vision involves exploring the uncharted and making your way. You'll discover resources, opportunities and support you could have never imagined.

Commit to being true to yourself. Screen your choices and your options by asking "Is this living true to myself?"

Allow yourself to value and consider all arenas of your life. Cultivating your self and your relationships with others is as important as your work in the world.

Consider how your gifts, interests and talents relate to the greater good of society. All of us can make a difference, and most of us want to.

Vision, Purpose, Values and Work

- *Vision:* Our ability to see new possibilities and make them real. Vision is our creative capacity.
- *Values:* The essential themes and patterns that run through our lives and actions that distinguish who we are. Values provide identity.
- *Purpose:* Why we are here. Our sense of mission and direction. The thrust of our lives. Purpose provides meaning.
- *Work:* The way we express our personal purpose in the world. The actions needed to make vision real. "Work is love in action."

THE RELATIONSHIP BETWEEN PURPOSE AND VISION

Purpose

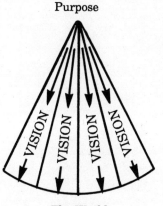

DIAGRAM 3:3

The World

CHAPTER 4

The Wisdom of the Heart

Love is honoring the sacredness of the human soul.
—UNKNOWN

In exploring what vision is, I have said that vision lives in the heart. You may be wondering what I mean when I talk about the heart? Am I talking about the physical heart or am I talking about the heart as a spiritual concept?

The heart I am referring to is both the physical organ in the chest and the spiritual essence or quality the heart represents. As the physical heart functions to keep the body alive, so the metaphysical or spiritual heart keeps the spirit alive.

The physical heart ensures that the cells of the body are nourished and cleansed, bringing nourishment to the cells of the body and carrying away wastes. Nourishment is drawn from various sources in the body including the lungs and the digestive system, while waste is transported to various places in the body including the lungs and the kidneys for disposal. The heart connects to every cell in the body by orchestrating the flow of resources to and from each cell.

The metaphysical heart also orchestrates nourishment. Through the heart we give to others and receive from others. Through the heart we heal, cleansing our spirits and our psyches by disposing of hurts, losses and beliefs that no longer serve us. When our hearts are open, we take in what we need. When our hearts are closed, we starve. Through the heart we connect with ourselves, with others and, ultimately, with the rhythm of life.

Emotions have both a physical and feeling dimension. When we experience sadness, for example, heaviness and emptiness can be felt physically in the chest. When we are happy, we feel light and buoyant.

Just as the physical heart is multi-chambered, the experience of the heart is multi-dimensional with many layers and capacities that unfold gently. The open heart runs deep, providing an experience of the unspeakable—of connection, peace and timelessness—a oneness with all of life. Many cultures recognize the profundity of the heart, giving it different symbols—the lotus in the East and the rose in the West.

A variety of people answered the question, "What is the heart?" by sharing their thoughts with me.

> The heart keeps the body alive. My heart tells me when I really don't like something, when somebody hurts me. Usually I'm lively. When I'm hurt, my heart feels different. It slows down.
>
> I get a different feeling in my chest. It feels kind of empty. My heart skips a beat when I'm scared.
>
> — Joshua Steele White, student

> The heart is the center for grounding and receiving—giving us meaning or purpose, making it last, giving it value. If something doesn't touch the heart, it is forgotten.
>
> — Jan Rarity, homemaker

> The heart is the essence, the soul or spirit, that inner and outer self that transcends space and time, the sensory moment. The essence of the heart continues after the body dies. The heart compels us to live with vision, aware that there is something much greater of which we are a part. This awareness gives us the desire and the ability to look for something much greater. The looking for something greater is what vision is.
>
> — Mark LeDoux, consultant

> The heart is where you test whether what you're visioning is right or not. For me, it's a kinesthetic sense. I know some-

thing is right because I feel it physically in my heart. When something feels right I experience a matter of fact kind of feeling, a reassuring kind of feeling that's nice to know. It's the kind of feeling that makes you say, "Thank God that's right!"— a sense of relief.

> —Clyde Hager, president, Neuro Dynamics, Inc.

The body as temple, the heart as gateway

Another way to look at the heart is as a *gateway*. You've probably heard the saying, "The body is the temple of the soul." The heart is the gateway in the temple. An open heart connects us to our soul (who we are at the truest, most essential level), our passion (our life energy) and to our creativity. This openness enables us to feel complete and connected with ourselves and others and expresses love, compassion, desire and a sense of possibility. A closed heart cuts us off from our own vitality and the love of others.

What Is the Wisdom of the Heart?

What does the wisdom of the heart mean? When you look for information or knowledge you may not think to look to your heart, yet the heart is your source for information essential for living with vision.

The heart knows what is true. In the moment and over time, the heart knows what is right. This includes both what is right for you individually and what is right in a larger sense. Your heart knows what is really important, what really matters. To be true to yourself and to others you need to listen to your heart.

The heart is the place of choice. The heart opens and closes. It says, "Yes, I really care," "Yes, I choose to stay," "No, I really don't want this." The heart's choice allows you to commit, to maintain and to be fully present. The heart gives permission to embrace and be embraced. The mind can help evaluate the choice and translate it into action. The will mobilizes the energy of the body to support the choice and move you into action. However will and mind, while powerful, are incomplete without the presence of the heart.

The heart is the source of creativity. Knowing what is possible, seeing beyond the limits of the current moment, the heart tells you how you truly want things to be. It provides a spark, an impulse, an inspiration that initiates creation. The spark is fueled and sustained by your passion.

The heart is the source of a sense of timing. It knows what speed is right for you. Your pulse is your inner timeclock and connection to the rhythm of life.

The heart strives toward wholeness. Both loving and experiencing love allow you to feel connected and whole. The rhythm of loving and being loved which the heart participates in is almost as instinctual as breathing in and out.

The heart coordinates all the parts of your being. A decision made without including the heart is not a complete choice but an imposition or a decree from the heart or from others.

The Place of the Heart in Living with Vision

Living with vision is living your daily activities from the heart from one moment to the next.

Listening to the heart requires:

Being able to find your heart. How often do you actually notice where your heart lives? Become aware of its physical location and how it feels.

Learning to quiet the mind. Let the mind become still so you can hear your heart speak. Often your head is cluttered with the sounds of many different voices, some judgmental, telling what you should and shouldn't do, what you should and shouldn't think. The commotion may not allow the heart's voice to be heard.

Learning to understand the language of the heart. The language of the heart is different than that of the mind. Gentler and more compassionate, the heart speaks the language of an artist—full of textures, sensations, images and feelings—often more qualitative than quantitative. We often discount the heart's commentary as foolish and unrealistic. It takes an open mind and a desire to hear in order to understand what is being said.

Feeling safe. The heart is vulnerable and doesn't want to be hurt or attacked. If in the past the risk of speaking and opening has lead to hurt, your heart will be quite cautious. You need to feel safe with and trust yourself to listen to your heart. You also need to feel that you are in an environment where it is safe to be vulnerable.

Being patient. Your heart doesn't always speak on command but when moved to. You need to be open and attentive to listen when it has something to say.

Finding Your Heart

Preparation

Choose an environment that feels safe. Get into a comfortable position. Close your eyes and give yourself enough space to breathe. Allow your breath to enter through your nose as you inhale, move down your throat and fill your belly, gently bringing nourishment and support to the cells of your body, letting each cell take in just the amount of nourishment and support needed in its own time and space. When each cell feels complete, return the nourishment and support you provide back out through your mouth as you exhale, only to have it return to you with your next inhale as the circle of your breath completes itself. Take a moment to let yourself become more familiar with the circle of your breath.

Exercise

Whenever you feel ready, find your physical heart in your body. Take a moment to notice where your heart is located and feel your heart beating in your chest, your pulse beating in your arms and in your hands. Let yourself become more familiar with your own heart, your own heartbeat. How does it feel right now? Distant? Present? Heavy? Light? Playful? Serious? Empty? Full? Take a moment to notice however your heart feels right now.

Then very slowly and gently, at your own pace, take a deep breath, bring your focus back into the room, and open your eyes.

Make some notes on:
1. What was this exercise like for you?
2. What observations did you make about your heart?
3. What did you learn in doing this exercise?

On listening to the heart:

> If we don't listen, the heart doesn't talk to us anymore. We need to listen to the heart when we have to face decisions. Our hearts can tell us if we want to stay on Earth or space. My heart keeps telling me, "Let's go up in space!" I think the world would be a better place if people listened to their hearts. I don't think that people know that listening to their hearts can be worthwhile. If people like presidents looked deep down in their hearts, they wouldn't want to bomb other countries or have troops out there killing people.
>
> —Joshua Steele White, student

> A lot of Einstein's theory came to him as a kinesthetic feeling. After he felt, he wrote it down and then went and worked out the formulas.
>
> —Carol Flake, associate professor
> University of South Carolina

> The heart is the essential core where the creative impulse comes from. The impulse starts as something bubbling up inside me and turns into an emotion seeking description and expression. As I need to describe it or express it, I begin engaging my mind. When I have an alive exchange with someone it's like a dance—connecting with someone and then responding. The response comes from the heart. The mind helps put things into words. There is a balance between leading from the creative impulse and engaging the mind.
>
> — Linda DeHart, integrative artist/designer

Trusting the heart can be difficult because of the fear of hurt. A split is made between head and heart to protect you. The head judges feelings and evaluates your environment, guarding the delicate and vulnerable heart. Because the head provides a sense of being in control, you are more comfortable trusting your head than your heart. You need to recognize that there is a place for both heart and head in living with vision. The head can support the heart in expressing your vision and making it real. The heart is the source of the creative impulse and the place of connection with the vision. The power of the impulse can be frightening. You need faith to follow your heart. Trusting the heart is easier when your mind cooperates.

Living from the heart is difficult to do because it doesn't make any rational sense. It takes a lot of courage. Society wants reasons. It's hard to do things without a reason and trust myself. It's a living trust or a living faith. It's a faith that's grounded in experience—trusting and having things happen, having things work out over and over again. Yet, each time it's still trust, it's still faith, it's still a risk. You never know for sure how things will work out.

— Jan Rarity, homemaker

It's hard to trust the heart because its message is unstructured and intangible unless the mind begins to take part in the structuring and differentiating. I have been to both extremes— too much structure and only trusting my heart. Neither one feels right. The way I naturally operate is to lead from the heart, from the creative impulse, and then to consciously use my mind to express it, to move forward into action. It has led me to understand what balance means. It's difficult to trust my heart when I'm not connected with all parts of me, my whole being.

— Linda DeHart, integrative artist/designer

Living from the heart requires a constancy of vision. The constancy can be difficult to sustain because the dream we are creating is not always there in a form we can recognize. The constancy goes away only because we have become so attuned to people telling us the dream isn't possible that we start to doubt the dream. People have told us since childhood that things are impossible. While our society tells us the dream is a mirage, often the reality is the mirage. The dream may be more real than what we call reality.

— Richard Jordan, healer to the legal profession

Living from the heart requires:

A belief in the incomprehensible. There is much that we limited human beings are incapable of understanding, such as the heart, vision and God. We are compelled to believe in these things even though we can't comprehend them.

Experiencing life moment to moment. This means living without remorse or guilt from the past or fear of the future and recognizing that the only moment that matters is the present moment.

Not fearing death as well as understanding that death is not the end. You can't live fully until you've dealt with the inevitability of your own death. Living from the heart requires acting out of love, generosity, unselfishness and forgiveness.

Clarity about what we want each moment of our lives. Life offers a number of choices every moment including the choice to live. Living from the heart requires that you be in touch with what you want and then choose what you want over and over and over again.

Willingness to change. Outer events change most people. In life change is a constant. It's part of being alive.

— Mark LeDoux, consultant

The Heart and Creativity

Michael Ray of the Stanford Business School and the author of *Creativity In Business* has found that creative people live from the heart.

People being creative:

Have an enormous faith in their own creativity.... [They] have] confidence. They really expect things to happen.

Have an absence of this inner voice of judgment.... [They] have an ability to shut down that voice that's saying, "You can't do that—you'll make a fool out of yourself....Your family will be out on the street—you'll lose your job.... It won't work.... You've done crazy things like that before." People doing business from the heart aren't listening to that voice....

Are living from their hearts.... [They] are full of wonder.... They observe things, everything, in a very precise way. They really pay attention to everything that's going on. It's that kind of curiosity that you have as a child that gets knocked out of you. It's that curiosity that pushes that voice of judgment aside....

Ask questions. They're always asking questions about things. It's another thing you have in your childhood that you don't seem to carry into your adult life.... It's so refreshing to get a question from the heart ... a question that's open and naive....

Are meeting the challenges of life. They're not going off to live alone in a cave.[1]

Vision Without Heart

Although having a vision without heart is possible, I would want to find another name to describe this kind of vision. At first glance distinguishing them may be difficult: both kinds are full of desire, emotion, passion and power. Both visions can be made real. There are two major differences.

First, vision with heart creates results which are in the best interest of all those it affects. Vision without heart creates results that harm the visionary, other people or the environment. Second, the process of making the vision real has a different quality. The process of realizing vision with heart respects the truth and integrity of all those touched. This kind of vision empowers others, attracts through inspiration and leaves all involved feeling whole. Vision without heart focuses on the desired result without considering the consequences for everyone. Vision without heart defines power as something you give and get rather than as a resource you have naturally that you express or withold. Heartless vision attracts by seduction, leaving those involved feeling empty, dependent, depleted and powerless in the end.

Vision with heart expands to include the personal visions of those involved. Others' visions are considered sacred and essential—part of the whole. Vision without heart is opportunistic and does not care about personal visions, except to attain a desired outcome. People are won over to a team and must buy into someone else's vision.

Vision with heart considers all those touched as interconnected, interrelated, interdependent parts of a larger whole. If all are considered, everyone wins. Vision with heart relies on the participation of others through free choice. Vision without heart considers people as "pawns on a chessboard." This is the game where there are winners and losers. In this sense, vision without heart involves manipulation.

The main character in the book *The Soul of A New Machine* by Tracy Kidder is portrayed as a man obsessed in his pursuit of a vision: designing a new computer product for his company. While his quest is successful and his story both dramatic and exciting, the way he attains his desired outcome can be questioned. He enrolls whomever he needs to make his project work and drops them when no longer useful. Vision with heart is not manipulative but compels us to relate to others with integrity and respect. Vision with heart is passionate without becoming an obsession. Obsessions eat us alive. Passions keep us alive.

Hitler is an example of someone who lived a vision without heart. He was motivated by a hunger for power and control more than a desire for truth. He was disconnected from others and his efforts resulted in the senseless deaths of countless people. Vision with heart never causes such violence or violation.

How can you identify a vision with or without heart? These questions can help. Listen to the answers your heart and your gut give you.

1. *What is the vision's underlying motivation?* Truth or power, service or accomplishment, love or fear? Vision with heart is motivated by truth, service and love.

2. *What impact does the vision's achievement have on others?* Are they full or empty? Better off or worse off? Vision with heart enriches those it touches.

3. *Does the vision inspire or seduce you?* Vision with heart inspires feelings of expansiveness and fullness. Vision without heart plays upon a deep-seated need or hunger and makes you dependent.

Carol Flake suggested another method. "Think of the vision and ask 'Is it love? Is it truth?' If the answer is *no*, the vision dissolves. It the answer is *yes*, then it's vision with heart."

Living from the Heart: The Place of Feelings

The heart and emotions are often confused. The heart experiences emotions but is more than the emotions alone.

When we are emotional, we experience feelings. In our culture deep feelings are often experienced as uncomfortable. When we have strong feelings we feel a need to "do something," often not knowing what to do. You want them to go away, to stop bothering you. Pushed away, feelings are no longer uncomfortable.

What you resist is sure to persist. Ironically, resisting feelings gets you stuck and prolongs the tension and discomfort you are trying to avoid. As you remain stuck in the feelings they have a power over you, and you become reactive. Your behavior feels base and out of control. You find yourself "reduced" to behavior that is habitual and automatic, and you may not even be aware of what you are doing.

The heart is not reactive, but open. Feelings move through the heart without getting stuck. In order to feel connected to the heart, you need to learn how to stay with your feelings. This includes gentle feelings and intense feelings, pleasant feelings and unpleasant feelings, feelings of joy, pain, longing, fulfillment, despair and connection. The heart can then respond rather than react. The difference between a response and a reaction is the element of conscious choice. A person who responds is making a choice to do so. When you react you are not able to make a conscious choice—you are a creature of habit.

How can you become more familiar with your feelings?

Give yourself permission. Human beings have feelings of all kinds—some pleasant, some unpleasant. To be fully human is to experience the full range of feelings.

Know that there is a difference between acknowledging feelings and acting on them. Often we are afraid to feel anger for fear we will be violent. Ironically, we are more likely to be violent when we don't let ourselves feel angry. Feelings are a current of energy passing through the body. If we block the path the energy gets trapped and seeks a way out sooner or later. If the energy, the feelings, are allowed to flow no action may be necessary. To feel them may be enough to give feelings permission to just be. If action is still necessary, choose to act consciously.

Create a safe space and become more familiar with your feelings. Experiencing deep sadness in the presence of a caring friend may be easier than alone. If you are afraid to be angry at a person, get angry at a stuffed animal, a pillow or a picture. Create an environment where you feel safe from criticism, interruption or insensitivity. To be vulnerable you need to feel safe. Many people choose to learn how to feel and express their feelings in therapy.

Become curious about your feelings. As a feeling is coming on or moving through you notice how your body feels. What parts of your body feel anger? What parts feel sorrow when you are sad? What parts of your body feel joy when you are happy? Allow yourself to watch and notice how you feel physically.

If you find yourself resisting feelings become familiar with the resistance. Give yourself permission to let the resistance just be there for a moment. Notice how you react physically— where you feel the resistance. Ironically, it is resistance to our own resistance, fear of our fears, that keeps us stuck and hurting more than the feeling of resistance or fear alone. Making it okay to feel scared or resistant allows the feeling to move through you and pass.

Give yourself space to breathe. When we are scared, anxious, angry, sad or even happy, we often forget to breathe. Breathing helps us relax, slow down, become more aware of the present moment in time and feel deeply and fully.

On Resistance

Why do you feel resistance? The heart seeks wholeness and movement. When you are moving too fast, moving too slowly or moving when you need to rest, resistance is a signal that your movement is off course. You may not be listening to or following your own natural rhythm. In this sense resistance can slow down, repace or renegotiate your movement, helping you find a more natural pace. The heart asks us to live and move in a way that is true to ourselves.

When You Are Feeling Resistance

Exercise

Get into a comfortable position. Close your eyes and take a deep breath. Give yourself enough space to breathe. As you inhale, feel the support the back of your seat is providing for your back, the seat of your chair is providing for your legs and tailbone, and the floor is providing for your feet. As you exhale, allow yourself to sink into your seat, letting go, letting the seat support you.

Whenever you feel ready, let your focus move to your heart.

Find your physical heart. How is it feeling right now? Let yourself simply notice. As you stay with your heart, allow yourself to focus on the resistance you are feeling. What does it feel like? Where do you feel it in your body? In your head? Your neck and throat? Your heart? Your solar plexus? The center of your belly? Your legs and tailbone? Take a moment to become familiar with the resistance. Let yourself be with and feel it. As you inhale let yourself breathe into the place of resistance and exhale. Notice what happens. How does it feel? As you inhale again allow yourself to gently embrace the resistance, seeing it embraced by the warmth of your heart. Exhale. Notice what happens and how you feel.

If your body could move with the resistance, how would you move? Would you move forward or move away? Would you push against it or surrender to it? What part(s) of your body would you move—your chest? your back? your arms? your hands? another part? Take a moment to notice. Try moving whatever part or parts forward and away, pushing against the resistance and surrendering to it. Keep breathing as you move—letting yourself inhale and exhale. Notice how you feel. Keep moving until you feel ready to stop. Take a deep breath, once again noticing how you feel physically and emotionally, then very slowly and gently, at your own pace, bring your focus back into the room.

The quality of relating

A second difference between heart and emotions is the quality experienced when relating to others. Relating from the heart has a quality of depth and fullness that includes both your own feeling and the feeling of another person. An important distinction to make is the difference between being *self-centered* and *centered-in-self*.

The self-centered person

Self-centered people make us angry, because when we are with them there's no room for us. They are so absorbed in their own drama that it's as though we weren't even there at all.

Not only are you not there to the self-centered person, but also they aren't really there either. At their core self-centered people feel wounded, incomplete, as though something is missing. They may not even realize this consciously. If they do they may not have any idea how to receive the hope, love and nourishment so desperately needed. The self-centered person is afraid to look inside, afraid they may find "nothing" there, a void. To face the nothing is so fearful that the person habitually moves away from this place of darkness.

In denying this emptiness the void becomes a vacuum, sucking in whatever passes without the element of conscious choice. In the presence of a self-centered person we feel the force of their inner vacuum, become drained, limited, controlled or powerless. You may feel cautious or afraid of a self-centered person, because there is no space for your needs and no respect for your personal boundaries.

Self-centered people are aware at some level that their relationships with others aren't working, yet they have no options. They are not insensitive, feeling the resistance, rejection and judgment of others, but don't know how to behave differently. While they come across as confident, underneath they are needy. They are as judgmental of themselves as they think others are of them. What they need most is love and self-compassion. The self-centered person needs to be loved and accepted at a very fundamental level. Their inner child may never have experienced the kind of love they truly need and may feel a level of pain so deep that the heart has been closed off. In order to develop the capacity for self-love, the self-centered person may need to first experience love and acceptance from another.

> Denial of pain takes a lot of energy and requires the person to bankrupt himself mortgaging his fears. And when you divert your energy... you don't have it where you need it— you might not have much of it at all.
>
> Many people push a burden of inexplicable sadness through a lifetime without ever gaining an understanding of the promptings of their hearts.[2]
> — Merle Shain, *Hearts That We Broke Long Ago*

The person who is centered-in-self

The person who is centered-in-self is a person everyone loves to be around. Such people strengthen our own sense of self. They are fully present to us; there is plenty of room to relate to them—the freedom to move closer or remain distant, to respect the needs of the other person and honor our personal boundaries.

Being centered-in-self comes from self-knowledge and self-acceptance. People centered-in-self have felt their own wounds, embraced their own darkness and filled their void with compassion and love. Having felt pain and sadness they have found peace and joy. Their personal journey has taken them through the darkness to the light of self-love and understanding.

Empathy and Sympathy

The difference between relating from the heart and from the emotions is the difference between empathy and sympathy. Empathy is a quality of the heart, a feeling of compassion for the other person, an experience of the pain and emotion the other person is feeling which creates a profound connection with them and a deeper understanding of who they are. Empathy is being present with the other person in the moment, accepting them and acknowledging their experience. As we heal our own wounds and become centered in ourselves, we develop our capacity for empathy.

In sympathy we focus only on the feelings of the other, losing our objectivity. We feel sorry for or badly about the other, separating ourselves from them or losing our sense of self, becoming overly absorbed in their feelings. Sympathy can involve distortion as we are not fully connecting with the other or with ourselves. Empathy goes much deeper than sympathy and provides a fuller, more authentic connection.

The heart's energy

The heart's energy is expansive. It is inclusive, not exclusive. As the heart opens and deepens there is more room for others, not less. Love flows in a circle from our hearts to the hearts of others, then from the hearts of others back to our own. As you open your heart and learn to receive love you become more alive, more fully engaged in the natural rhythm of life.

Woundedness and vulnerability

At some level we are all wounded. All suffer or have suffered from a broken heart. Whether in our childhood or adulthood, whether through intent or innocence, all of us have felt abandoned, betrayed, invalidated or simply invisible. Having been denied what is most basic and essential to live and to grow, our hearts become frail and vulnerable. We lack the strength to protect ourselves and build impermeable walls around our hearts to provide protection from further hurt. Our hearts close, numb and harden as though they were stone not human flesh. No one can touch you. While you avoid feeling your pain, the impermeable wall keeps out the love you really need and prevents the wounds from healing.

Healing your sacred wounds requires courage, care and patience and is essential to living with vision. If your heart is closed, you can not connect with what matters and what you care about. You need inner strength to let down the wall that defends your heart and still be protected. In the presence of someone who really knows you, with whom you feel safe and understood—a friend, a lover, a gentle therapist—you can begin to heal your wounded heart. As you feel the pain the heart opens, allowing in the needed and previously denied love and nourishment. Feeding the heart with love strengthens it, making it safer to open and creating inner protection. The familiar wall dissolves, becoming a semi-permeable membrane that acts as a screen or a gatekeeper, helping the heart discriminate what should enter and exit. The membrane allows in the love you need to thrive and keeps out people and situations who would do you harm. Vulnerability takes on a different quality—one of safety and openness rather than danger and loss. A healthy heart wants to give and receive, to love and connect.

Carol Flake's metaphor of the oyster and the pearl beautifully illustrates the place of wounding and healing in human growth:

> When I think of living with vision, I get an image of an oyster. The beautiful pearl the oyster grows begins when the oyster is wounded by a grain of sand. As our hearts are wounded we close down our shells around them. When you've been wounded it's scary to open your heart. Now when the heart

opens up it wants to close down to avoid experiencing the wounding. Yet if the shell is closed the heart suffocates. Through love the human spirit is kept alive. Through wounding people grow and develop, like the oyster and the pearl.

Healing

"Only the wounded can heal."
At least only the compassionate
Can know what healing is about
And only the wounded can know
How deeply, deeply healing is needed.
After being wounded again and again
And fiercely pierced
And walking in utter loneliness
Through dark nights and bright days
For ever so long
One learns
Enough
To know in one's heart
What healing is not.
Healing has to do with union and reunion
Reconnection
Re-creation
And becoming whole.
Risking the exquisite and horrible
Vulnerability of intimacy
And intimacy of vulnerability.
Healing is walking with another
On life's journey
Being together
Through suffering, change and growth.
Healing is the depth connection
Representing
God in each of us
Deep within ourselves
And through the vast universe
Always available
For us
Just as are some people,
If only we will come
Out of hiding.[3]

—Carolyn Treadway

Natural Rhythm: The Rhythm of the Heart

Many of us live our lives trying to keep up with the pace of the world. This world says work is from 9 a.m. to 5 p.m. Monday through Friday; Saturday and Sunday are free. This world says vacations are 2, 3 or 4 weeks a year if we are lucky. You wake up to alarm clocks, look to a wrist watch and mechanical clocks to monitor your progress. You compare your actual progress with what you think you should have done given the elapsed minutes, hours or days. In this sense, you are looking outside of yourself to establish the pace for your life.

Rarely do you consider that you have an inner timeclock. Just as the physical heart is the pacemaker in the body, the heart in all its facets (emotional, spiritual and physical) is the pacemaker for your life. Your pulse, your heartbeat, is your own natural rhythm. The rhythm of the heart can tell you how fast to go, how slow to go, when to go and when to stop. The heart can tell you what to move toward and what to move away from, what is true and what really matters.

When your heart feels heavy or sluggish, it's time to slow down. When your heart feels full and energized, it's time to move forward. Stress may be understood as the tension you feel when your capacity to respond is out of alignment with the demands you perceive from your environment. The further you are removed from your own natural rhythm, your own pace and capacity, the greater the stress you will feel as you try to respond to environmental demands.

Finding Your Own Natural Rhythm

Your pulse, your heartbeat, is your own natural rhythm. You can find it anywhere in your body since your pulse beats everywhere. Your chest, your neck, your arms and your hands might be good places to look. Just close your eyes, take a deep breath and begin to notice your pulse beating in your chest, neck, arms or hands. Take a moment to become more familiar with your pulse's own natural rhythm. Notice the pulsations moving in and out, back and forth. Let yourself become familiar with your own rhythm, your own pace. Give yourself enough space to breathe. See if you can quiet your mind. Do you find your heart and your head have different paces? Listening to your heart requires stillness and time.

The Pace at Which You Live

Exercise

Get comfortable, close your eyes, take a deep breath and relax. See if you can find your heart, and take a moment to become a little more familiar with it, noticing its beating in your chest, your pulse beating in your arms and your hands. Focusing on your heart, take a moment to look at the pace of your life right now. Is the pace too fast? Too slow? Just right? Take a moment to listen to your head's response. Now ask your heart. Once again, take a moment to listen. Are their responses similiar or different? If so, notice how.

Once again, take a deep breath and relax. Ask yourself another question. How do you determine the right pace for you in living your life? Do you have an inner sense of pacing? Do you set goals based on the calendar? Do you follow the pace set by the organization you work for? Do you set your own pace? Do you follow a pre-planned schedule? Do you act on the whim of the moment? Do you think about your pace consciously? Take a moment to notice your responses, and just let yourself become familiar with them.

Take a deep breath, relax once again and ask yourself another question. Do you look to your heart when determining the timeframe for a project or activity? If yes, think of a time you might have done this? What was it like? What happened? How might you use your heart as a source of information about pace and timing? What does it mean to follow your heart?

Take as much time as you need to stay with the questions and to feel complete for the moment. Whenever you feel ready, take a deep breath and slowly and gently bring your focus back into the room.

Make some notes on the following questions:

1. How do you feel about the pace of your life right now? What adjustments would you make?

2. How is your head's sense of timing different from your heart's sense? How can you take both into consideration?

3. What does it mean to follow your heart? What pace would you set for yourself if you followed your heart?

Connecting with the Rhythm of Life

In addition to helping you discover and monitor your own pace, your pulse expresses your own unique note, your own rhythm in the larger rhythm of life. Your heart beats in harmony with the hearts of other people, with the hearts of groups of people and with the heart of the Earth.

Imagine that you are part of a chorus which comprises all beings who live on this Earth. Each creature's heart sounds a particular note in a particular rhythm. When all come together, a chorus is built of all these rhythms and notes. Imagine singing in this chorus. Find your own note. Hear the sound of the chorus. Now experience the sound of your own note and that of the chorus both at once. How does this connection feel? See if you can feel the vibration as your heart resonates with the hearts of others. The resonance creates a feeling of rightness, a feeling of belonging, a sense of coming home. Notice how your note resonates, vibrates with those of the whole chorus.

You may find it hard to hear both your own note and the sound of the chorus. To get lost in yourself or lost in the chorus is easy. Many of us lose ourselves in an energetic, exciting larger group. To experience being part of the group and also true to yourself, you need to be centered.

The following exercise can be done in a group of any size to help you become familiar with the relationship of your own natural rhythm to the rhythm of the group and to expand your awareness of your connection with the rhythm of life.

Finding Your Own Natural Rhythm

Exercise

This exercise can be done sitting or standing. Arrange the group in a circle, with each person an arm's length apart from the next.

Close your eyes, take a deep breath and give yourself enough space to breathe. Follow your breath as it enters through your nose, fills your belly, bringing nourishment and support to all the cells of your body, letting each cell take in the amount needed and returning the excess back out through your mouth as you exhale, returning the breath to the source from which it came only to have it return to you once again with your next inhale. Take a moment to become more familiar with this circle of your breath.

Whenever you feel ready, allow your focus to shift to your heart. Where does your heart live? Can you feel the beating in your chest? Can you feel your pulse beating in your arms, in your hands? Take a moment to let yourself become more familiar with your pulse, with your own natural rhythm.

Next, allow your focus to move to your left hand. Allow yourself to feel your pulse beating in your left hand. Let yourself become more familiar with it. Whenever you feel ready, reach out your left hand to your neighbor on your left. With your right hand take the hand of your neighbor on your right. Keep your focus on your left hand, on your own pulse, on your own natural rhythm.

Notice your neighbor's pulse beating in your left hand, beating in counterpoint with your own pulse. Allow yourself to notice each rhythm, to notice the two of them beating together. Imagine that these are two notes in a song—a melody and a harmony. How do they sound alone? How do they sound together? Take a moment to notice this.

Now imagine that the rhythm, the note, of your neighbor enters through your left hand, moves up your arm with your own pulse and enters your heart where you add your own note, your own natural rhythm; and then send the two notes on and out through your right arm, through your right hand, passing them on to your neighbor on your right. Imagine your neighbor adding his or her own note and passing these on and on and on until everyone in the circle has added their own note, their own rhythm. Imagine what it sounds like to hear all the notes, all the rhythms, sounding together in a chorus. Take a moment to notice the sound and the feel of the chorus; and notice your own note, your own pulse. What does it feel like to feel both your own note and the sound of the chorus?

Imagine that the rhythm of the heart of the group is beating in harmony with the hearts of many other groups of people in your city, in your country, around the world, and that these hearts are in turn beating in harmony with the heart of the Earth. Take a moment to feel these connections. Can you feel a sense of energy in your own body, flowing through you and around you? Through connecting with your own heart, you can connect with other people, with groups of people and with the heart of the Earth.

Take a moment to once again become familiar with your own natural rhythm, your own pulse, and whenever you feel ready very slowly and gently take a deep breath and bring your focus back into the room.

The group can discuss:

1. What was the experience like?

2. Could they feel the energy of the group? What did this feel like?

3. Could they feel both their own rhythm and the rhythm of the group? How did that feel?

4. What can the group learn from this awareness?

The Dance of Life

For years I've wondered how my love of dance and singing related to my work as a healer, facilitator and social entrepreneur. I knew only that singing and dancing made me feel whole, creative, alive and connected with myself and the rhythm of life. The more courageous I have been in healing my heart, the better I've come to know myself, the fuller and clearer my voice has become. Like magic. My voice comes from the depth of my soul as I open my heart. I become an instrument, letting life flow through me, through my body. When I dance I feel fully alive, joyfully celebrating the gift of life. Life works if only we let it. Life asks each of us to live as singers and dancers, becoming intimately familiar with our bodies, our voices and the roles we have to play. As we master our own instruments, we'll find ourselves playing in the dance of life. As we heal our hearts and live as the people we truly are, we can live fully, experiencing life as a continuous celebration.

PART II

Living
With
Vision

CHAPTER 5

Embracing
the Dark

When we face the dark side, we are dying.
Our concept of who we are is dying.
Our perspective and experience of who we
thought we are is dying.

—*MICHAEL JARO*
PSYCHOTHERAPIST

The foundation for living with vision would not be complete
without including a part of life that is easier to ignore: the
dark side.

Facing the dark side is the most challenging, grueling and
also enlightening part of living with vision. Often I've felt
angry, frustrated and beside myself as my inner landscape
and outer circumstances grew bleak, empty and grey. Whether
at a loss for words, impatient with my efforts or simply feeling
lost, I have come to know the dark side intimately while
writing this book. Although painful and uncomfortable, these
times have yielded some of the most powerful insights in this
book. The dark night of the soul is both an end and a
beginning. Nature works in cycles and darkness is part of
nature. As a friend reminds me, "From the womb of winter,
spring is born."

The dark side is not a struggle between good and evil but an
invitation to gain a deeper understanding of our inherent
wholeness. Embracing the darkness is a gateway to growth in
a lifelong search for purpose and meaning. The dark side of
experience forces you to ask yourself questions about who you

are and how you are living your life. Crises force you to let go
of habits, beliefs and possessions that no longer serve you and
to search inwardly for answers, for insight and, ultimately, for
truth. While the heart-centered perspective of conscious/
compassionate people assumes darkness is part of wholeness,
society does not. Our rationalistic society cuts us off from vital
parts of ourselves. As we hit our limits—what we don't have,
what we can't do, what we don't know—we develop compen-
sating mechanisms. That addiction is such a public topic
today is not surprising. In a world of isolation and separation,
we are starving for love and connection. Addictive and compulsive behaviors are desperate attempts to fit ourselves into
a fragmented reality when cut off from the love we really need.

As a workshop leader and therapist, I have listened to many
stories of encounters with the dark side of life. Facing the
darkness is critical to living with vision. In the words of Merle
Swan Williams, "People who have been through crises are
able to define visions and patterns more easily because they've
been forced to learn to see and to seek."

Facing the Darkness: A Story

Moments in the darkness are often critical turning points.
When I was sixteen, a violent experience turned my life
around. Attacked by a stranger and believing I was very close
to death, I made a commitment to my purpose. I had been
aware of my life purpose from the very beginning, but had
been afraid of my own power and the responsibility that came
with being who I truly was. I had been running away.

I was attacked in my own neighborhood at night as I walked
home from work. The experience was surrealistic, as though
I was in the audience in a comfortable seat watching myself
play the starring role of victim in a drama.

The moment of truth occurred as my attacker attempted to
strangle me. I had used up all my physical and mental ability
to stop him. My life was on the line. I had to make a choice:
Would it be to live? I didn't know. Then a voice inside of me
screamed, "I want to live!" "Let go," another voice said. I let
go. "All right, God. All right," I surrendered. "If I live, I'll own
my purpose. I'll embrace it. I'll live. I'll really live!" Out of the

silence came an inner voice. "Forgive him!" instructed the voice. Without a moment's hesitation, without thinking, I found myself telling the man, "I forgive you," speaking calmly, offering peace and love.

As soon as I spoke, my attacker burst into tears. "I don't want to do this," he moaned. "I don't have a choice." He told me I was not his first victim. He had been in jail for murder and rape. He'd escaped prison, but life had no escape. While strong and brutal, he was also delicate, fragile, broken. He had nowhere to turn.

For a moment there was silence, just silence, he was breathing deeper as he lightened his hold. I wondered if it was over. No sooner had I thought I might be free than his mood changed back to violent anger. As he prepared to beat me once more, I again let go inwardly. At that moment a car came driving down the alley where we were. My attacker ran off into the darkness. I had been given the gift of life a second time.

The experience pressed me up to the limits of my fears then offered me an invitation to fully engage in life. While the circumstances were both dramatic and violent, ones I would never wish to repeat nor wish on anyone else, I can see in looking back that my encounter with the dark side facilitated my relentless purposefulness today. Only in facing death could I fully know life.

Friends and clients who have had near-death experiences tell similar stories. We think it's death we fear; in truth what we fear is life. To be who we are, to acknowledge our personal purpose and place in the world, to live from our own truth is more fearful than exposing ourselves to the dark and the light which are intrinsic to nature and life.

Another lesson I've learned from the dark side: The obstacles we face are in proportion to the contribution we are making. It is when I'm doing my most important work that I face the most difficult obstacles. The obstacles test me and my relationship to what I am doing and propel me forth as I show that I am truly committed.

What is the Dark Side?

The linear perspective has framed the dark side in terms of good and evil. Evil is understood as an inherent limitation, an inability to live up to potential, a conscious or an unconscious desire to harm. To this way of thinking the dark side is the opposite of the light—something to be avoided and feared. Evil is understood as a powerful force that takes us over, turning us into what we most dread and fear.

Today the thought of the dark side evokes terror in most of us. We resist and reject it; we fear and deny its reality. Life, we believe, is supposed to be light and easy. "Good" people experience "good" feelings. Love, trust, happiness, giving, and serving are all "good."

"Bad" feelings are dirty and often inappropriate. If you feel them, you are supposed to suppress and keep them to yourself. To be fearful, desperate, hungry, lonely or angry is not okay. This is both our myth and the reality of our society. No one wants to face the dark side of life.

The dark side of life is inevitable. We all have moments of darkness. Try as you may to avoid, escape, deny or ignore it, pain pursues you. To the degree you resist, the darkness grows stronger. Struggle and resistance leaves you tired and powerless. Sooner or later you have no choice but to let go and experience the dark side.

The dark side has many faces and many names. It includes moments of uncertainty, loneliness, feeling empty, feeling nothing or feeling afraid of feeling nothing. The dark side may be a bump or an obstacle you stumble over as you move along your path or an abyss into which you fall—a seemingly endless, bottomless, black hole. Often you don't see it until you are in it. Called the shadow, the void, the abyss, the nothing, lack of meaning is a major part of the dark side. Your beliefs are being shattered and you don't know what to do. As you struggle to regain control, you find you have nothing to hold on to. Resist as you may, you feel like you are falling into "the void."

The dark side evokes terror. In the darkness you feel afraid, helpless, powerless, lost and out of control. The strength of these feelings can be overwhelming, causing you to disconnect from your pain and so from your own experience. Many of us numb out psychically, physically and emotionally to avoid facing the crisis of meaning underlying our pain.

The dark side can be experienced physically as well as emotionally. It can bring a hunger, an emptiness, a chronic loneliness in our hearts, our guts or our solar plexus that never seems to go away. You may experience the dark side physically as an emptiness or void.

The darkness may appear in what seem to be favorable circumstances. You may plunge into the abyss. When you meet a person who is everything you've ever dreamed of only to have them disappear suddenly and abruptly; or you interview for the ideal job, make it through three sets of encouraging interviews, then never hear from the company; or your careful investments (on which you've built your future) fall through just when you are ready to use them as planned. No matter what you do, your efforts seem futile. Things feel out of control, and so do you.

The dark side accompanies loss. What you lose can be internal (your health, sense of self-worth, longstanding beliefs, a dream) or external (a job, a relationship, a home, an opportunity).

The dark side teaches that you are not in control. You want to be. You try to be, but you can't be. You're not in control; life is. To the degree you try to resist or control life, you hurt and you fail.

Addiction is a symptom of denying the dark side. You try to run from feelings, circumstances and people who are too frightening or painful. You run to work, relationships, money, smoke, drink. You numb yourself and overcompensate through addictions to processes (working, making money, having sex) or substances (alcohol, drugs, food). You try to fill the void rather than experience the void. In your pain and discomfort, you desperately grasp at straws. You are really denying your inherent wholeness. Eventually you learn you can't get enough of something you don't want. What you want more than anything is to feel your life has some meaning.

"Losing Everything to Have Everything"

Marion is a woman who has learned that the darkest times make way for better times.

I lost everything during the period from 1975 to 1976. I had been very successful: good job and career path, plenty of money, a relationship. I thought I had it all. So did everyone else. I lost it all: my job and my primary relationship. I walked around the streets with five dollars in my pocket—all I had left.

For almost three years, my attempts to make sense out of what was happening to me failed. Every time I tried to use my old pattern of coping, the one that had made me so successful before, I failed. Whether looking for jobs, taking steps to improve my financial situation or any other attempt to move forward and take action, I would get sick or something wouldn't work out.

This period taught me great humility. I felt tremendous despair and depression, and was overwhelmed. I didn't know I had that much despair in me. It slowed me down. It forced me to be with my experience, to stop doing things myself, to let people help me, to let go of my supercompetence and workaholism. It forced me into the depths of darkness. The *do-aholic* side of me kept going until I finally understood that this wasn't the way. When I let go, I had a new way of living and being, a new outlook, new options.

Help comes from the most unimaginable sources when we are open. Closet angels or teachers are everywhere. Two of my greatest teachers were a gum-chewing, street-wise waitress and an uptight accountant who told me, "You have a great gift to give—go out and use it!" I didn't quite know what this was, yet I moved on. My sense of work began to evolve. It led me to a new career that has brought me success and respect. It was a very grueling, painful time and a very rewarding one. I had a good therapist to help me through. My life made a quantum shift. I now see, in retrospect, that it allowed me to open, through a healing process, to a different sense of wholeness, to where the source of empowerment lies.

What Purpose Does the Darkness Serve?

Our world asks us to look outside for answers that can only be found inside. Defining success, sense of self, goals and aspirations by using other people's standards distances us from ourselves. The dialogue between our inner selves and the messages around us becomes unbalanced. The outer voices take over in a monologue that offers no space for deep thinking or authentic feeling.[1]

External standards make you less certain about who you really are and curtail expression of your natural talents. As you inhibit your true self and spirit, you are reduced to focusing on survival—food, shelter, clothing and your most basic needs. You build a fortress of protection—a home, relationships, financial security, position—against the more primal, natural aspects of life. Have you ever felt frightened when meeting a person who lacked this protection—a homeless or destitute person on the street? We don't like to see people who are this vulnerable as they remind us that no one is immune to the rough tides of life.

Living fully brings vulnerability, uncertainty and not knowing, moments of pain and emptiness as well as moments of richness, fullness and true joy. The depth and intensity of feeling that come with aliveness evoke fear and terror. Underneath the terror is a yearning for a stronger sense of self, a sense of purpose and meaning, an experience of being seen and feeling connected. As thinking people we're caught in the middle of a fight between mind and matter: The body wants the truth to emerge; the mind wants to push it away.

> Your willingness to wrestle with your demons will cause your angels to sing. Use the pain as fuel, a reminder of your strength. It's like walking down this strange road that's the landscape of the self. You simply have to be willing to confront whatever you discover there. It's all a process of discovery. What happens all too often is that we run from the parts of ourselves that we least recognize. You have to be willing to stand up to that and push beyond it.[2]
>
> —August Wilson, playwright

The darkness compels you to accept your humanness. In this sense, darkness is a gateway to yourself, to an understanding of the human condition and to the nature of life. Only in facing the darkness do you gain true compassion for yourself and for others.

The darkness helps you rediscover the parts of yourself that are buried. The angry lion discovers the part of him that is a gentle pussycat. The gentle pussycat becomes the angry lion. People discover that they are multi-textured, multi-faceted creatures, and very much the same at heart. You need to feel what's missing, to discover and create what you want and need.

The darkness breaks down structures that are not working and no longer serve you. Nature instinctually recycles what is dead, letting decaying matter provide fertilizer for new life. Rain forests grow out of soil that is rich with volcanic ash. The dark side tears apart old beliefs, relationships and ways of living to create space for new growth and learning. Your psyche and your life are renovated so that your truest self can be more fully seen and expressed. You discover who you really are in contrast to who you think you have to be.

Facing the darkness builds a new respect for self and for life. You learn that "life works." This can be called faith: It provides a foundation for embracing and pursuing your heart's desires and dreams. Embracing the darkness makes you take yourself more seriously and live more purposefully.

"Broken Heart, Vacant Dreams"

Maria has great potential to live as a visionary. Her mind is rich and full of feelings, images and textures. She perceives her life and experiences through a magical lens that captures every sense, every detail of the moment. She has a gift of making the ordinary activities of daily life come alive. I am struck by the pictures she paints of her experiences, as though she were directing a movie with her words. When I ask her what she wants or what her dreams might be, her vivid mind empties. She closes down. "I can't do this," she says. She gets angry. She withdraws.

I have asked her many times. Her response is always the same. How can a woman who is so richly graphic have no words, no ideas, no images to express her hopes and dreams?

As I've seen the pain she carries, the distance she keeps from her intimate feelings, from her heart, I have come to understand why her dreams are vacant. Her heart is broken, kept in chains. Something happened long ago, maybe many somethings, so painful she shut the door to her heart.

I don't believe that she doesn't have dreams, but that she can't let herself look at them. To her dreams are futile because they are outright impossible. Dreaming is hard with a broken heart. The fortresses of protection she has built around her heart keep her from living fully, being happy and expressing herself.

This woman does not lead a heartless life. She is a very loving person. However, her ability to live the depth of her desire, the depth of experience she is truly capable of, is limited. "I am hungry in a way that feels insatiable," she tells me. "No matter how much I eat, I'm never full. The hunger never seems to go away. I want to feel satisfied. I want to live fully. I know that something is missing. Something is wrong."

In her search for fulfillment, trying to fill the void she finds inside her chest when she looks for her heart, she is discovering her own dark side. Inside of her is a little girl who doesn't really know what it is like to be loved, accepted or valued for just being who she is.

Until you have embraced and felt the darkness, you are limited in your ability to hope and dream. We all go through the "dark night of the soul" in order to become fully who we are and can be. Most of us walk around with broken hearts, hearts that have been battered or enchained. Numb, we neither feel the heart nor listen to its warnings or its needs. We are afraid to trust the heart and let ourselves know what really matters. To live in denial, avoidance, or fragmentation is safer than feeling what we want and need deep inside our hearts.

In embracing the darkness, you feel pain, move through it, and develop an inner strength that never leaves you. You become less dependent on external cues and more self-sufficient. You discover that you are whole and complete. You develop a deep, lasting respect for life and experience the sense of awe or wonder you knew as a child when you discovered how something worked in nature.

Facing the Darkness: Finding the Void

As you face the darkness, sooner or later you find yourself feeling vulnerable, helpless, hopeless and powerless.

One man's wife—call her Susie and her husband, Sam—tells about his voyage into the void:

> When my husband was suicidal, he was afraid to look into the *nothing*, the abyss he felt caught in during the course of his depression. He'd get close to the edge. He'd almost look in, and then he'd turn away—until one day he let himself look. He let himself feel the abyss. And everything changed. Now, he's not so afraid. And even when it gets dark, he knows it will never be as dark as before. Now he knows there's a bottom to the abyss.

Facing the darkness includes three phases:

1. *Falling into the void: holding on for dear life*

With our lives out of control and the power to change things out of our hands, we have no choice but to fall into the void. We try our best to resist falling, afraid the fall will never end—afraid that the void has no bottom. In terror we grasp at something to hold on to, branches or ledges that will stop our fall. Work, money, relationships, an artistic pursuit, exotic travel and community service can either be sources of fulfillment or ways to escape falling into the void. While appearing to be constructive, when used as a crutch they become obsessions or distractions. We get hung up on the circumstance—lack of money, no time to find a new job, loss of an intimate relationship—and miss the deeper feelings, the real issue. Some ledges (alcohol, drugs) are both empty and destructive.

Inside our heads we are saying: "If only I had enough money, I'd be safe." Money becomes a ledge. "Perhaps money will protect me from falling into the void. If I get more money, I'll escape." So we work and work toward the goal of acquiring money. We may be successful or unsuccessful in that effort. Either way, the focus is a temporary distraction from our fall into the void. We appear to be moving forward, or at least treading water, rather than falling downward at a fast and furious pace.

Sooner or later the ledge breaks. Having attained money, we still feel incomplete. We find ourselves in a familiar place:

the darkness. Falling again and again we are terrified, searching for a ledge to stop the descent, to hold on to. Again we get
lucky; we find another ledge. This time it may be a relationship. "If only I had the right relationship, then I'd feel safe and
secure," goes the conversation. "Then I'll be protected; then I
won't have to fall into the void." We set off on a journey in
search of the right relationship, finding it or not, but at least
buying time, treading water. Again, sooner or later, with
another person or alone, we find ourselves feeling empty,
hopeless, purposeless and helpless. Once again we continue
our descent into the void. These behaviors are attempts to find
something to fill the void so we can walk across the abyss
safely—without feeling pain or entering the darkness. We
fear falling because we fear death. Ironically, this leads to an
avoidance of life itself. In life we fall many times, and in falling
we learn what we need to know in order to soar.

THE FALL INTO THE VOID

Falling   Finding ledges   Hitting bottom   Recovery

DIAGRAM 5:1

2. Hitting bottom: letting go

Sooner or later we become tired. The pattern—treading water, finding ledges, holding on—is wearying; falling becomes
all too familiar. We run out of ledges. Or we may find ourselves
falling so fast and furiously that we can't grasp anything along
the way. There's nothing we can do but surrender to the
current or, in a familiar saying, "go with the flow."

There is a bottom to any fall. We know when we hit there.
Our fall has left us torn and tired. We have no protection. At

the bottom there is nothing. In our weary state we have no choice but to let go, to pray, to turn our fate over to a higher power without knowing if there is one or what will happen. We are forced to be with, let in and embrace the darkness, to let the darkness become part of us and integrate it into our lives.

Surrender has a fairly negative connotation for many people—as though in surrendering you give up or lose yourself. Surrender, as I use it here, is not a giving up but an allowing. In surrendering we allow ourselves to be more fully in the moment and to embrace all parts of ourselves and to be embraced by a larger flow of life. Because we are afraid of the unknown we may resist letting go, even if we understand the place of the dark in the natural order of things. We don't have to like where we are. We simply need to find a place of acceptance or permission within us for darkness to exist.

The moment of hitting bottom may be a life-threatening event or one that shatters your identity or sense of self. As you hit bottom, there is a moment of recognition, a feeling of *this is it*. You may say to yourself and the powers that be, "I've had enough! I can't take it any more," or simply, "Stop!" You get your power back just as you give up control. You give up some of your old habits, limiting beliefs and comforts and **recover** your will.

Losing self to recover self

Gary's story is one of surrender and letting go. In facing the darkness, he appeared to lose his old sense of self while becoming aware of a greater sense of self.

> My encounter with the dark side began when a woman I was in a relationship with broke up with me. It ended suddenly. The reason, she told me, was that I was needy.
>
> During that time I experienced insomnia. I felt like I could cry every day. I spent two weeks feeling angry and enraged. I was disoriented. My mind became involved with obsessive thinking. I needed to know I was okay. The little boy in me wanted his mommy. I needed to be with people who would let me know what I was going through was okay.
>
> I wasn't myself. I kept asking myself, "Who am I?" I didn't know how to relate to people except through a false persona: Goody-Goody-Two-Shoes. I would come up to someone and say, "How are you?" I would tell them about my life, yet I

couldn't tell where I was. I didn't know if what I was saying was true. I would ask my friends, "Am I coming across to you? Am I real?" Usually they would say, "Yes."

I began questioning my work. I questioned the principles behind my professional training that I had applied so faithfully. I had nothing I could count on, nothing to hold on to. I could not hold on to my sense of self as a kind loving person.

I realize now in retrospect that the darkness was a doorway. I was going through a process of dying and rebirth. My concept of who I was, was dying. While first seeming like a monster, the dark side was a revelation. Through this death/rebirth experience, I came to know myself more honestly—to reclaim a part of me that had been split off.

3. Recovery: integration and moving forth

Once we have let go, given over our wills, surrendered and allowed ourselves to fully embrace the darkness, we begin a period of recovery. We find ourselves filled with new insight, feeling lighter and able to see possibilities that we couldn't even imagine before. We pick ourselves up, nurse our wounds, and may experience ourselves both stronger and softer than before our fall. We discover how deep we go and how many resources we have to draw upon.

We may take it easy for a while, yet sooner or later we find ourselves getting back on our feet. If we have fallen into the bottom of a canyon, we need to find our way back up to the top. The climb may be slow and wearing, yet each step along the way means that we have come through the worst of it. We are strengthened in knowing we have hit bottom and survived. As we climb, we find our vision clearer, our sense of self stronger, a greater respect for the force we call life. More aware of the resources within us, we find our sources of support more abundant. At the heart of our new awareness is an ever stronger sense of faith.

The recovery period is one of integration. This includes letting go of old beliefs and structures that do not serve us, be they relationships, activities, ways of thinking or objects. In letting go we experience loss, feeling empty and a sense of yearning. The emptiness and yearning create the space for new people, experiences, feelings and dreams.

Integration involves embracing parts of ourselves that we have not recognized in the past, parts which have been uncomfortable or even invisible. The tumultuous life circumstances and emotional upheaval that characterize falling into the void and hitting bottom are catalysts for meeting unfamiliar parts of ourselves and becoming intimately familiar with them.

Integrating the darkness involves living with paradox and forces our thinking to expand to include seemingly contradictory parts of ourselves. The notion of counterpoint in music is an example of how seemingly unrelated notes of music combine into a larger harmony. We discover that what appears to be unrelated or even opposite at one level is interrelated at another. We can both love someone or something and want to move closer while running away. We can be committed and still unsure. We can experience moments of doubt and still have faith. We learn to speak in sentences full of *both/and's* instead of *either/or's*. Many great geniuses, including Einstein, went through periods of great confusion on the verge of brilliant insight.

Having fallen into the void, survived and come out the other side, we discover humility, dedication and praise.

Humility: Think of humility as a process of becoming more fully human. Humility brings an appreciation of the magic, the wonder, and the nature of life. We realize that no matter how great, purposeful or powerful any of us may be as individuals, we are still small creatures in the ever-changing drama of life. To play our roles, we need to see ourselves as actors in this larger play.

Humility rightly gets a bad name when we try to become humble through discipline by telling ourselves we *should* be humble. True humility comes through experience after life knocks us around and shatters our beliefs, teaching us we are not in control and that life is a force greater and more knowing than we can ever hope to be.

Dedication: The kind of dedication that results from facing the darkness is a commitment, one that reaches deep and wide. This kind of commitment comes from learning how life works and choosing to accept it. There is a quality of surrender to this dedication, yet not the kind of surrender where you lose a part of yourself or give up something precious or essential. It is quite the opposite. Because facing the darkness brings a deeper knowing and sense of self, we can let go without losing faith or connection with our power, desire or sense of self.

Praise: Whenever we get knocked over or threatened and land on our feet, going through the experience with our faculties intact, we experience a kind of lightness, joy and sense of gratitude that wells up inside of us and needs to be expressed. This appreciation makes daily living a celebration. Even when the going gets tough and I feel sad or afraid, a part of me remembers that I still have the precious gift of life. Praise is the experience of knowing our blessings and how good it is to count them.

Vision and the Void

To understand how the dark side relates to living with vision, notice how you feel when you ask yourself the question, "What do I really want?"

For most of us, one of two responses is familiar:

1. Fear of the dark stops us from even asking the question. The conversation inside may go like this: "I don't know what I want—and I don't want to know," or "I can't answer the question—I'm too frightened," or "What good does it do to look at what I want when I can't have it?"

2. We think of wishes and dreams in fairy-tale terms. They have a magical quality quite removed from the harsher realities we know to be life. We don't take them seriously. We tell ourselves: "It's just a whim—a wild fantasy and not very realistic" (implying what we want has nothing to do with reality and it isn't worth considering).

In both cases we discount our desires as impossible or foolish, distancing ourselves from our hearts and our deeper selves. Facing the void brings us closer to our vision, to the things we want and desire because we are brought closer to our truest selves. We open up. We are forced to look inside and to learn about ourselves. We are forced to appreciate and take more responsibility for our lives.

In learning more fully who we are, we learn both our limits and our desires. Our vision becomes clearer, as does our understanding of what we need. Knowing what we want and what really matters, we become more purposeful. In being purposeful, we choose a course of action that is both inspired and realistic. We feel more focused, truer to ourselves, more directed and more connected to the essence of life.

Alone, Yet Not Really Alone

There is a difference between loneliness and being alone. When we are alone, we are with ourselves. When we are lonely, we are cut off from our own experience, from ourselves, and are unable to let others touch us. The more fully we can let ourselves experience ourselves and the situation we are in, the less lonely we feel.

Maggie, a visionary artist, has pioneered many new frontiers on her own. Her innovations have been more out of fate than choice. Seeing herself as a player in the larger play of life has given her strength to go it alone when no one seemed to be there.

> I've had a gift I've wanted to give the world for many years. It's the gift of myself. I give it through my work as an artist and through the way I live my life. I have experienced many times where I give my gift and it is not received. In fact sometimes it isn't even recognized. This has been quite painful. It's like throwing a treasure into a deep, empty bottomless pond. There's no reflection in the water. It's like not being seen, as though I am not even there.
>
> My response has been to take it upon myself to do what needs to be done and not wait until I've felt welcome or supported by others. I couldn't wait, because I couldn't count on others being there. I've been disappointed. I've felt lonely—like there's no one who understands, there's nobody else out there.
>
> I have had to learn patience—to hold my gift in the highest light and not to give it so fully until the ground is prepared for the gift to be received. I have also needed to shift my perspective. I do what I can and realize there's a larger plan. I'm just one contributor. So I stay with my contribution and continue doing what I can. Yet it's a different level of doing than before. I realize I am part of something greater; and though at times I may feel alone, in my heart of hearts I know that what I am doing is not separate from the rest of life. It is a part. I am connected.

The Road to Vision:
What It Is and What We Expect It To Be

As we set out toward our desired destination or vision, we find there's an open space between where we are and where we want to be. This is what I call the GAP.[3] We think of the GAP as a straight line which leads us on a clear path from HERE to THERE. We follow the path putting one foot in front of the other, and while taking a step forward is sometimes difficult, at least we feel safe in knowing where we are and where we are going.

As we walk along the path, however, there are moments when we don't move forward, backward either or even stand still. At these moments, we lose our balance and lose our footing entirely. We find ourselves falling, not down, but downward into uncharted territory that doesn't fit our understanding of getting from HERE to THERE.

The GAP, we discover, isn't a straight line but has depth and width like a canyon. This is the void. We expect to walk along solid ground and find ourselves walking on a tight rope across a dark canyon. If we lose our footing, we don't just fall on our faces or behinds and pick ourselves up. We fall off the tight rope and into the void. (See Diagram 5:2.)

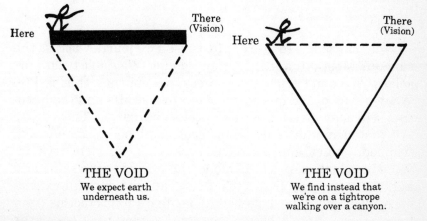

WHAT WE EXPECT

Here · There (Vision)

THE VOID
We expect earth underneath us.

WHAT WE FIND

Here · There (Vision)

THE VOID
We find instead that we're on a tightrope walking over a canyon.

DIAGRAM 5:2

As we lose our footing and fall, we are terrified. The stakes are higher than we ever imagined. In fact, treasured parts of our lives are at stake. It's like being the stakes in high-risk dice game, with our reputations, savings, job or relation riding on the outcome.

The journey toward vision is always different than we can imagine—richer and more unpredictable, a series of highs and lows, occasional plateaus, a constant string of new experiences. A picture of the journey as we actually experience it might look like this:

THE JOURNEY TOWARD VISION:
A SERIES OF UPS AND DOWNS

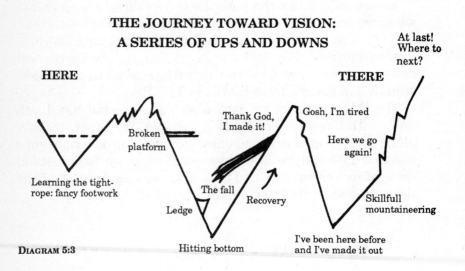

DIAGRAM 5:3

What causes us to lose our footing as we journey across the canyon? Most often it is fear and doubt. We don't trust ourselves. We don't trust the process, the journey that is life. We're afraid of the unknown, of our own limits and the harm that will come to us if we can't protect ourselves. These fears are rooted in the real life experience of being abandoned, trapped, judged and wounded. From this experience we develop beliefs that we are all alone, the world is not a safe place and we can't trust ourselves. As we survive painful experiences, we create our beliefs and our fears to protect us from future harm. Beliefs become habits that may limit or trap as well as protect us. When limited by our beliefs, we lose the ability to view each moment as unique and to choose how we wish to respond moment by moment. Our reactions are predictable. While initially life's circumstances may have been dangerous, the fear itself becomes dangerous, keeping us from adapting and responding to life.

Given the perceived danger of the journey, the fact that many of us never set out toward our visions in the first place is no surprise. Some who have set out might never have started if they had realized that instead of a solid linear path, the journey is like walking a tight rope across a canyon.

In spite of the danger life has a way of compelling us to be adventurers or mountaineers. Our spirits crave adventure, learning and growth, and compel us to be graceful acrobats and skillful mountaineers. We learn to walk the tight rope. If we fall into the canyon, we learn to climb back up in our own time and manner and get on our way. We emerge humbler, wiser, stronger and more committed to getting where we want to go. People living with vision while facing great dangers reap greater rewards than they ever imagined when they first set out.

Getting started on the journey is difficult. In time, life helps or forces us to venture forth. The journey begins as we choose to embrace life and be who we are, to give up hope and act on faith; to give up control and let ourselves be guided. When we give over our power to a higher power, we find ourselves empowered. We each begin in our own time and in our own way. Having started, sooner or later we will be where we want to be. There is power in choice and intention. How we get there and when is part of the mystery of life.

The Place of Pain in Living with Vision

Living with vision is both joyful and painful. I asked colleagues to tell me about pain in living with vision. Here are their thoughts:

> Pain is resistance to what is. When I accept it, pain softens and has a whole different texture and quality. Pain is a significator and makes us look. When you put a square peg into a round hole, it tells you something doesn't fit. You need to look at it.

Pain moves you into something you're not looking at. If you're in enough pain, you have to give up control of life. We seem to think life is on our terms—that we're in control. In this way we are separate from life. We live in a dualistic world. Pain says we can't lie about the way things are. It moves us into the truth that we are in a world of separation. Pain makes us admit what's true.

—Michael Jaro, psychotherapist

Pain is an imbalance, sometimes emotional, sometimes physiological. Pain is an experience that has been there. When we re-experience it, we become vulnerable. It opens us up. We feel this vulnerability and openness in our bodies and in our emotions. The experience of the newness and the unknown shows up as pain.

In the experience of living pain, an unfolding and discovery process takes place. The pain can be an instigator of growth. In feeling your pain there's a sense of relief or possibility in the body and a discovery of strength emotionally. In the process of experiencing pain you discover new strength in yourself.

—Elizabeth P. Valentine, massage therapist

Pain brings truth into being. It's different in every case.

—Catherine Cooper, consulting director

People who have been through crises are able to define visions and define patterns more easily because they've been forced to learn to see and to seek.

—Merle Swan Williams, social entrepreneur

Pain serves to help us learn. By suppressing pain we try to bypass experience. People get identified with pain—addicted to it or addicted to the quick fix. When we don't leave space for growth, which is a natural instinctual need, we perpetuate pain.

—Margo Schmidt, psychic counselor and consultant

Creativity is very connected to pain. Out of the seeds of darkness our vision and our creativity can be born. They can help us see more deeply where our own true desires lie.

—Lisa Wexler, teacher, counselor, artist

Embracing the Darkness: How to Do It

I don't know that it ever gets easier to feel the emptiness, the pain, the yearning in our darkest moments. I do know that attacking the darkness with the force of will only leaves me battered and bruised.

When I feel vulnerable, unsafe and unprotected, if someone senses my emotional heaviness and asks me to lighten up I only become more frightened. On the other hand, if someone comforts, listens and attends to the little girl inside me who is frightened I lighten up automatically. Listening and accepting without judging washes away the darkness, provides safety, and opens us to be who we are.

Both our language and our techniques for dealing with the dark side tend to incorporate will and force. We talk about overcoming obstacles rather than acknowledging them, about bypassing or escaping rather than being with them. Obstacles can be teachers if we learn to listen. If we embrace them they dissolve before our eyes. They are transformed from barriers into gateways offering new possibilities.

Here are some suggestions for embracing the darkness:

Give yourself permission not to know, not to understand. All of us experience times when we just don't know. You only suffer by thinking you *should* or *can* always know.

Choose a loving environment to be in where you feel comfortable and safe. You may want a particular physical environment: home or away from home, indoors or in nature. You may want music or silence, someone with you or time alone. Looking through old photographs, favorite poems or letters, can help remind you who you are and what really matters.

Decide whether it is better for you to face the dark side alone or with another. Sometimes, no one can take away the feelings of pain, loss or grief. At times like these another person's presence becomes a way to avoid the darkness and fill the void we feel inside. On the other hand there are times when in facing the darkness alone you become a martyr. You empty yourself beyond empty. You don't know what to do. You hurt intensely yet are stuck in the pain. At times like these you need to take the risk of turning to another person and asking for help. Trust yourself to know what you need.

Become familiar with your feelings. Our culture separates us from our feelings, physical and emotional. We live in our thoughts. Feelings are uncomfortable, especially when they are unfamiliar and intense. As you embrace them, physically and emotionally, they are less powerful.

Ask yourself what about your current situation you might not be seeing. What isn't working? What else might be present that you haven't seen? What else might you do? These are questions to ask gently and lightly. If you don't know the answers it's okay; they will come. It's only by asking and being open that you will come to know.

Spend time in silence in meditation or prayer. Sometimes our lives are so busy we live in constant commotion. Only in silence can you listen to the voices inside of you and what they have to say. In silence your mind learns to be quiet so your heart can speak. Running, swimming, dancing, hiking and other physical activities also can provide opportunities for meditation.

Explore your connection with a higher power. Facing the darkness builds your capacity to experience God, nature or life itself. As your spiritual connection deepens you are better equipped to face the darkness.

Darkness and Society

This chapter has focused on the dark side in our personal journeys. Not only do individuals face the darkness, but so do groups, organizations and society as a whole. If we examine the reality of life today look at the issues facing us, we are living in a time of great darkness. At the global level we are confronted with huge problems: hunger, violence, the threat of nuclear war, AIDS, the depletion of our natural resources, an impending breakdown in the world's monetary system. You know the long and familiar list. We face the darkness in our personal lives and in our organizations: the confusing roles of men and women; the struggle between balancing family and work life; creating a work environment that encourages creativity yet operates efficiently; the fallout from acquisitions, mergers and the stock market crash; increased stress and job dissatisfaction.

Groups, organizations and society are comprised of a web of individual people. We are all part of the larger environment in which we live— both affecting and being affected by it. The concepts, stories, questions, and models included here for the individual relate as well to the dark side in groups, organizations and the larger society. The specific issues may be different, however the underlying questions the dark side asks us about our group's identity and purpose are the same.

Individually and collectively we can face the darkness and integrate it into our lives. This will lead to restructuring how we live and relate. In restructuring our society we will come to view outside forces as indicators or change rather than as dictators.

Evolving to a New Species: Tearing Away the Ego, Revealing the Soul

As we evolve from thinking to conscious/compassionate people, there is good reason to believe that a new species is evolving. In the process of evolving, we are experiencing a reforming or restructuring of the human ego. The results are now appearing both in individuals as physical and emotional changes and in the way new organizations are structured (see Chapter 9, Humanizing Organizations).

At the root of this evolution is the change in our egos. As thinking people, we find the ego has brought us a sense of self accompanied by defenses and structures to help us live, relate and survive. The ego has also brought rigidity to our thoughts, feelings and physical form. While these rigidities or habits once protected, they now limit us.

More and more people are experiencing a ripping or tearing away of the ego, forcing them to reveal their inner selves, the delicate fabric of their very soul. As we evolve to the concious/compassionate stage the ego gains a spiritual dimension, allowing us to be flexible and responsive, rather than rigid and reactive.

The process of ripping away the ego is emotionally painful but can also be experienced physically as well. I have felt this tearing in my heart, my solar plexus, my belly and my genitals, both on the surface and deep within. The ripping and tearing is a process of uncovering our most essential selves. In the process we experience the pain and terror of our vulnerability. Integrating our experience frees us. My heart, my solar plexus and my belly have become more solid as the shift has taken place inside me. The ripping and the tearing lessen.

As I evolve, my faith grows stronger, my creativity bursts from me and my comfort with the unknown increases. I feel more connected to myself, to other people and to the rhythm of life. I am at peace more often and able to trust my intuition to guide me. At the thinking stage creativity has been associated with productivity, particularly the mind.

As conscious/compassionate people we will discover that creativity comes from embracing all parts of ourselves and learning to orchestrate rather than manipulate. As we develop a willingness to embrace the whole, we will find ourselves better equipped to handle the issues we are facing as a world as well as those in our individual lives. As we know ourselves better we become more purposeful and responsible and can create sustainable ways of living for ourselves and for our world.

CHAPTER 6

Living
With Vision

Your daily life is your temple and your religion.
Whenever you enter it, take with you your all.
— KAHLIL GIBRAN

The art of living with vision is incorporating it into daily life. To consider lifelong dreams and what you really care about for a weekend or to take a workshop and be transported into the world of possibility is wonderful. But somehow the dreams evaporate when we re-enter the everyday world. The endless demands of work, family, friends and the unexpected command our constant attention. We lose touch with our dreams in our effort to stay afloat in the rapids of day-to-day living. And yet, daily life is where vision becomes more than a dream.

Being able to simultaneously remember my vision and respond to the demands of the situation at hand has been my greatest challenge. I wish there were rules that could tell me just what to do, yet each moment, each situation, is different. There is no formula for the process of living with vision. The reality changes every moment and is different for every individual. Living with vision involves knowing yourself intimately—emotionally, physically, mentally and spiritually.

While I cannot offer "answers," I can describe the guidelines that I've developed for myself. Creating a lifestyle and quality of life that supports what I care about is a great foundation for living with vision. This includes time for reflection as well as action, taking care of myself physically and emotionally and allowing other people to support me. Often the only thing I know for sure is what I care about, and the only step I know how to take is the next one. Over time I have learned as well that this is all I need to know at a given moment. My sense of direction comes from what I care about. The next step gives me concrete action to take. Over time the sum of all my small steps is substantial. The golden rule of living with vision is: *All you need to know is what you care about deeply and what your next step will be.*

Creating a Lifestyle that Works for You

The quality of my lifestyle, the way I live every day, is the most essential part of living with vision. My physical surroundings, my support system, the pace I set and the way I care for myself all are essential to my health, my outlook and my general well-being. Quality of life (how I live) is different than standard of living (what particular material things I own). My quality of life is my foundation enabling me to do what I need and want to do. As I have gotten to know myself more and more intimately, I have created a way of living that supports my true nature.

Here are some questions that can assist you to create a lifestyle that works for you:

What you need
- What is essential to you; what can you not live without?
- What matters most to you?
- What makes you happy?
- What does a high quality of life mean to you?

Your living environment
- Where do you enjoy living? (By the ocean? Near the woods? In the city?)
- What colors do you most enjoy?

- What kind of physical environment makes you feel comfortable? (A large open space? A cozy room? A light-filled room? A shady corner?)
- Do you like to live alone; do you like living with others?
- What does your living environment need? What makes up your personal touch?

Your support system

- What kinds of relationships do you need?
- Special friends you care about?
- Supportive friends who care about you?
- Intimate friends with whom you can share your feelings and thoughts?
- Steady companions you can count on, who are really there for you?
- Collaborators who share your values?
- Facilitators who can coach you, help you sort through a situation and look at your next steps?

Self-care

- What nourishes your body, your mind, your heart?
- How do you communicate emotionally, mentally and physically?
- When and how much time do you need to yourself?
- What is fun to do?
- What is meaningful for you?
- What relaxes you?
- How do you balance reflecting and doing?
- What time do you naturally get up in the morning?
- What time do you naturally go to sleep?
- What pace is most comfortable for you?

Considering all of the above and any other qualities important to you, what would you need to create a workable lifestyle?

Practical Meditation

In an action-oriented culture, taking it easy, relaxing and reflecting are hard. Meditation is reflection, relaxing and letting go, a technique to open up your heart to the deeper parts of yourself, opening yourself to a place of deep connection with all of life. For many meditation seems strange or foreign, what a Buddhist monk does in an isolated temple, not what busy people do who live in the "real world".

I will try to demystify meditation so you can see how to include it in your daily life. Just as a car has different gears that you can shift in and out of, people have different levels of consciousness or awareness. Usually you run around in high gear, busy, racing against the clock, putting out lots of energy. When you meditate, you shift gears, slow down, let go of time and space and move deeper into yourself. Just as sleep replenishes the body after a long day, meditation rests and energizes you as you move through the day. Meditation enables you to quiet the constant chatter in your head, to learn to be still and relax. While daydreaming, fantasizing or spacing out can put you in a semi-meditative state, to enjoy quality life you should learn how to reach a meditative state consciously. A key to meditation is developing "the observer" inside. The observer is curious, attentive and non-judgmental of the sensations, feelings, thoughts and images you experience in your body. The observer simply watches what's going on inside and says, "Isn't that interesting? My that's curious." The observer is good at asking questions and patient at waiting for responses.

To become more familiar with your "observer," close your eyes, take a deep breath and let yourself relax. Allow your mind to quiet and focus on your breathing, air coming in through your nose as you inhale and returning back out through your mouth as you exhale. Let go for a moment of the need to understand, judge or put meaning on your experience. Just notice what's happening inside of you. Is your head talkative? Quiet? Are you tired? Energized? Are you tense? Relaxed? The observer will notice, "My head is quite talkative right now. As I pay attention, it quiets down. I'm feeling tired, but closing my eyes and taking a break feels good. I'm pretty tense, but I'm getting more relaxed." Your observer simply reports information seen and experienced like a researcher or journalist. You may want to practice getting to know your observer.

You can shift from high gear into a meditative state simply by closing your eyes, taking a few deep breaths, relaxing and letting your mind quiet. You may want to focus your attention on your breathing or on your heart. As you meditate more often, you'll find your observer appearing quite naturally, your focus moving inward, your heart opening and whatever questions or insights you need to know appearing.

Meditation can be done in many places:

Your office. If you have some moments of privacy, no one will notice if you close your eyes for a few moments.

Your car. You won't want to close your eyes while you're driving in traffic! However you can take some deep breaths, relax and let your mind quiet while driving on the highway.

Your bed. Giving yourself some extra time between waking up and getting out of bed in the morning is a wonderful way to start the day. I give myself half an hour or so, whatever time my body needs to gently move from sleep into a waking state.

The shower. A warm shower can quiet your mind and help you relax. Notice how the warm water feels as it touches your body, the texture of the soap and the smell of the shampoo.

The bathtub. This may be even better than the shower, since it's more relaxing and one tends to stay longer in the bath than the shower.

Doing household chores. Any repetitive task is a good context for meditation. You can keep your mind focused on the rhythm of a rake going back and forth or dishes being washed, rinsed and put aside.

On the tennis court, dance floor or running path. Exercise provides wonderful space for relaxing the mind, feeling connected to the body and reflecting.

Regular meditation increases the bursts of creative insight both during and after. This practice also helps me stay balanced, centered and alert as I go through the day.

Developing a Vision: How Can I Do It?

Creating a lifestyle that works for you and establishing a regular practice of meditation are good foundations for living with vision. Here's what's involved in developing your vision.

Step 1: Opening to the vision

Give yourself permission to ask what you really care about
and want. Allow yourself the space and time to look and
discover. The place to begin looking is in the heart. Ask
questions and listen for answers. Sometimes there will be
stillness, quiet, nothing. Sometimes there will be rich images,
feelings and sensations you can't put into words; other times
an abundance of words will pour forth. What's important is to
develop an organic process. Vision has its own sense of timing;
as long as you cultivate your vision and have the patience to
let it evolve in its own time, your vision will grow.

Step 2: Grounding the vision

Grounding the vision translates the heart's language and
experience into a form the mind can grasp. This includes recording your thoughts, images, feelings, questions, insights
and ideas on paper in words, pictures and colors, and talking
about your evolving vision with others. Both techniques in
communicating your experience clarify what your inner reality is.

Compare what you want with the situation at hand. See
clearly what could be and compare that with the way things
are. This helps you identify what action you need to take to
make the vision real. You can see the vision in a larger context
and determine what is most important and needs to be done
first.

Step 3: Choosing the vision

The next step is moving from exploring your vision to actually
living it. You do this by choosing the vision. See the vision
clearly and say, "I want this. I choose it." Make a commitment
to have what you want. There is enormous power in taking a
stand for yourself that enables you to mobilize your energy for
taking action.

Step 4: Taking action

Taking action is how you use this energy to make your vision
real. Taking action involves taking your next step and then
subsequent steps, one by one, asking yourself each day, "What
needs to be done? "and "What can I do now? "Action means

finding resources you need. Action includes seeking and getting the support you need to keep going.

Step 5: Reviewing, acknowledging and adjusting

This step involves asking: "Where am I going?" "Where have I gone so far?" "What have I accomplished?" "What have I learned?" "What adjustments do I need to make?" See how your vision has changed, give yourself credit for what you have done and learned, and decide what to do next. Rarely do visions develop according to a plan. You can set goals you want to reach and identify milestones along the way; but also learn to expect the unexpected and adjust your plans accordingly, keeping in mind both the purpose and vision of what you want.

Sustaining a Vision

Sustaining vision over time takes a lot of inner strength. There will be days when what you want seems so elusive or hard to get. Every day you need to choose the vision and hold the choice deep in your heart. I can feel hopeless, not knowing how to create what I want or what to do next, and still choose to live with my vision. Holding a vision is like holding a baby that needs support and room to grow. Holding a vision is a balance of holding on and letting go. You will probably hold on too tight or too loose at first before you learn where the balance point is.

Living with vision is like a dance. In any dance, there are times to move forward and times to move back, times to move faster or slower and times to rest. While you can make conscious choices and take actions that support what you want, you need to work with the larger scheme of things, the rhythm of your life. In trying too hard to "make things happen" and to move more quickly than you actually can, you work against the tide and find yourself getting stuck.

Perhaps the hardest time to sustain the vision is when you are stuck. Yet each time you encounter an obstacle, a critical moment—living with vision is happening. Obstacles are teachers that introduce you to your current limits, to what you don't know or understand so that you can learn and grow. While frustrated by the limits and wanting to overcome them or push them away, you really need to become more familiar with each particular obstacle and learn what it has to teach. As you have more experience in facing and moving through obstacles, you learn how these challenges actually move you toward your vision.

Working with Vision: A Checklist

Each day:

1. *Give yourself permission to be yourself.* Ask what you really want and care about.
2. *Look into your heart.* Find out what really matters.
3. *Use your mind.* Translate your heart's desires into words, images, ideas, thoughts, symbols and actions, and record them on paper.
4. *Talk about your emerging vision with others.* Ask them for feedback.
5. *Compare your vision with the current reality.* Let your vision be complete, seeing what you have, what you want, and what is needed to move from where you are to where you want to be.
6. *Identify your resources.* Including people, information, materials, money and time. Start with who and what you know now.
7. *Ask for help from others.* Who can support you? What roles can they play? What do you need to feel supported so you don't have to do it alone?
8. *Choose a focus for taking action now.* What is your next step? Identify one that is clear and possible to do today or tomorrow. Choose something you really want to do rather than something you think you should do. Decide when you'll do this and choose to do it.
9. *Take your next step.* Follow intention with action.
10. *Review your progress.* Celebrate your accomplishments. Learn from your obstacles. What can you learn from what has happened? What is there to do next? Set your next goal and continue on your way.

11. *Balance your time between reflection and action.* Some days the best thing to do is take it easy. Other days you will be all charged up and ready to run.
12. *Learn your own natural rhythm.* We each have our own sense of timing. Trust your instincts.

Where You Are Right Now:
The Lifescan—An Inner Photograph

The following technique can help you look at where you are in your life right now in relationship to where you want to be and can enable you to take the pulse of the different parts of your life and of your life as a whole. You will explore each part for a split second, as though you were a photographer who captures the essence of where you are at a moment in time. This technique can be used both as you set out to develop a new vision and as you review your progress.

Preparation

This exercise is a meditation. Try to record it on a tape or ask a friend to read it while you focus on your own experience. In addition to a tape recorder or a friend, you need the following worksheet and a pencil.

Exercise

Close your eyes, take a deep breath and relax. Allow yourself to get comfortable, following the flow of your breath in through your nose as you inhale, moving down your throat, filling your belly, bringing nourishment and support to all the cells of your body. Let each cell take in just the right amount of nourishment and support it needs. And when each cell feels complete, return the excess back to the source from which it came as you exhale through your mouth. Let the air return to you with your next inhale as the circle of your breath completes itself. Take a moment to become more familiar with the circle of your breath.

Whenever you feel ready, take a moment to locate your physical heart and see if you can feel it beating in your chest, in your arms and hands. Become familiar with your heart, your pulse, your own natural rhythm. Keep your focus on your heart, and when you are ready to move on take a moment to examine your relationship with yourself right now. How do you feel about yourself? Are you kind and loving? Judgmental? Angry? Become familiar with the way you are feeling about yourself right now. When ready, keeping your focus on your heart, open your eyes and make a mark on the first continuum on the worksheet. When done, close your eyes, take a deep breath and return to your heart, your heartbeat.

Continue to follow the same format for the next questions as follows:

- Focus on your heart, your pulse and your own natural rhythm.
- When ready, examine the question and take a moment to become familiar with it. Pay attention to your feelings on the subject as given by the few key words under the line.
- When you feel ready, keeping your focus on your heart, open your eyes and make a mark on the continuum on the worksheet. When you're done, close your eyes, take a deep breath, and return to your heart, your heartbeat.

After completing the first eight items on the sheet, proceed with the following:

When you feel ready, allow yourself to review the different parts of your life, your relationship with yourself, with others, your work, your purpose, money, your place in the world, your sense of spirituality, your relationship with change. See if one part of your life calls your attention most right now and if one does, take a moment to become familiar with it.

Whenever you feel ready, very slowly and gently take a deep breath, bring your focus back into the room, open your eyes, and make some notes on the ninth item of the worksheet.

The Worksheet

Date: _____

1. **Your relationship with yourself.** At this moment in time I:

Love, accept and cherish myself	Hate, reject and judge myself

2. **Your relationship with others.** At this moment my relationships are:

Intimate, nourshing
and fulfilling

Distant, depleting
and incomplete

3. **Your relationship with your work.** At this moment work is a place of:

Creativity and self-
expression

Drudgery, necessity
and obligation

4. **Your sense of personal purpose.** At this moment I:

Have a clear sense of
purpose. I dance with
life.

Do not have a clear
sense of purpose.
Life happens to me.

5. **Your relationship with money.** When I think about money, I feel:

At peace.

Uncomfortable.

6. **Your relationship with the world.** At this moment I feel:

I'm making a difference.

I'm separate from the world

7. **Your sense of spirituality.** My connection with God, a higher power, the universe or a life force is now:

Strong.

Not felt at all.

8. **Your relationship with change.** I feel that change:

Is a natural part of life;
I welcome it.

Gets in the way of
living. I resist it.

9. **Does any one part of your life call your attention** more than any other part of your life? If so, which part?

Where Do You Want to Be: Vision-Building

Vision is wholistic—what you want for one part of your life relates to what you want for the other parts and for your life as a whole. The following exercise enables you to build vision in any part of your life or for your life as a whole. After completing the lifescan you can use this to develop your vision for yourself, your relationships, work, money, your sense of purpose, your home or your life as a whole.

Preparation

Like the lifescan, begin with a meditation. You may want to tape-record the exercise or have a friend read to you as you close your eyes. You'll need a piece of paper or a journal and a pen, crayons or colored markers to record thoughts, images and feelings from the meditation.

Exercise

Step 1: *Choosing a focus for the exercise.* Do you want to explore your vision for your life as a whole? For one part of your life? Write down a statement that articulates your focus. (Example: "I want to develop a vision for my life as a whole and specifically, for a right relationship with my work.")

Step 2: *The Meditation.* Get comfortable, close your eyes and relax, giving yourself enough time and space to breathe. Whenever you feel ready, find your heart, your physical heart, and let yourself become familiar with your heartbeat and your pulse. Keeping your focus on your heart, allow yourself to review the focus you have chosen for this exercise. Allow the child within you to join with the adult you are. Then ask yourself, if you could create the life you truly wanted how would it be? What would you be doing? Who would be with you? What would your environment be like? How would you feel? How would your life be different than right now? How could you tell that you had what you wanted? See if you can create a symbol that represents what you really want. As if this experience were a movie, what title would you give it? Take as much time and space as you need to sit with these questions. Let your focus return to your heart, to your heartbeat, and let yourself once again become familiar with it. Whenever you feel ready, very slowly and gently, at your own pace, take a deep breath and bring your focus back into the room.

Step 3: *Recording your findings.* In your journal or on a piece of paper, make some notes about your vision. Include both what you found during the meditation and any thoughts, images, feelings that come as you write. Use pictures and colors as well as words.

Include:

1. Notes about your vision in as much detail as possible

2. How your life would be different from the way it is right now if your vision were realized

3. How you could tell you had gotten what you wanted

4. The symbol you created (or make one up now)

5. The movie title (or make one up now)

Step 4: *Grounding the vision.* Having started with the heart, here's where the mind comes in to flesh out the vision and to identify a course of action. In your journal, list:

- *A desired result you want to create.* Choose something you don't have now that you would have if your vision were realized. You may want to choose a timeframe for creating this result; if so, use your gut to do so. This may or may not turn out to be realistic as you go about the step-by-step process of making the vision real. That's okay. It's your best guess.

- *Qualities in yourself you need to draw upon to create this result.* What strengths do you need to call upon? What new qualities do you need to develop to make your vision real? Example: Faith, love, patience, perseverance, passion, commitment to having what I want, playfulness, presence, resourcefulness.

- *Resources you need to help you create what you want.* Resources are people, places, things, money and information. Include any questions you have about resources.

- *People who can support you and specific roles you can ask them to play.*

- *Your next step— one that is clear, realistic and doable today or tomorrow.* Choose something you *want* to do, rather than something you think you should do. Write down exactly what you'll do and when. Choose a friend you can share the step with both before and after.

Living with vision involves:

1. Continuing to identify and take your next step day by day.

2. Reviewing your notes that describe your vision and adding to or revising them as your vision grows and evolves.

3. Continuing to identify and find resources you need to realize the vision.

4. Asking for help and support from others as you proceed. You may need different kinds of support at different times.

5. Acknowledging and celebrating your steps and your accomplishments.

6. Viewing the process of realizing the vision as an adventure or a journey with many lessons to learn along the way.

Visions grow and clarify over time. You can do this exercise as often as you want to see how your vision evolves. What's important to remember is that living with vision is a natural process. The longer you live with the process, the more familiar it becomes. As you live with vision, you will find yourself determining where you are and where you want to go and identifying what resources and support you need to realize your vision each step of the way quite naturally. Your life overall will feel more purposeful and your daily life more complete.

CHAPTER 7

Managing Your Natural Resources

Everything about a person originates from the core of his being.
A person's body,... his behavior, his personality,
the way he moves, what he talks about, his attitudes, dreams,
perceptions, posture are all part of a unitary whole.
All are expressions of his core.
—RON KURTZ AND HECTOR PRESTERA
IN THE BODY REVEALS

Home is where the heart is. For years I didn't think much of this statement, viewing it as a platitude. While I wanted to feel at home in the world and found myself constantly seeking places where I felt welcome, my search seemed an endless one: looking and never quite finding what I needed.

One day I asked myself a simple question: "If home is where the heart is, where does the heart live?" "In the body—in the chest, Dummy," was the answer. "Wow," I responded. Obvious, perhaps, yet I had never thought about this. I had looked endlessly to find a place called "home" outside myself. Now I realize home is within, so wherever I go I am at home.

We also often look outside to find needed resources; rarely do we assess our inner resources. Many of us are afraid to look for fear there is nothing there since we have lost touch with our own most natural resource, the body. We live as though our heads were separate from the rest of the body which is often times considered base, dirty and primitive. After all, thinking people ought to suppress instinctual responses.

Our bodies are a vast frontier and an abundant terrain to explore. They are energy generators and a rich source of information. Our bodies are our homes, our temples.

Discovering Your Own Natural Resources: Bridging the Split Between Mind and Body

What are your natural resources? At work and in school we are taught to use the mind, in particular the left brain. The mind is one resource of the body. Others include intuition, energy and natural rhythm. Your energy is the most fundamental resource. Often you don't think about energy until you are tired, stressed out or ill.

In Chapter 1 we noted that in our thinking stage of development we have separated mind from body. We live by the credo "mind over matter." For many, physical experience ends where the neck begins. At work we sit passively at our desks or in meetings. We drive in our cars for hours on end. We treat our bodies like a burdensome piece of luggage, often cut off from our feelings and physical sensations.

The social drugs of our culture—coffee, candy, and junk food—further remove us from our natural physical sensations. We control our alertness and energy level with substances and stimulants. If only we would notice and listen to our bodies' signals we would find other, healthier alternatives. An executive who described plans for her new office told me, "I'm ordering a big, new couch. I get tired during the day, and I can lie down for 30 minutes or so to refresh myself. I hate not being alert." "Bravo!" I thought. Thirty minutes invested in rest and replenishment provides hours of increased energy and productivity later.

The price you pay for "living in your head" is a lack of awareness of many parts of yourself, a loss of self-expression and an inability to fully experience your life. You spend time going through motions, unable to experience and respond to what life presents moment by moment. Your body is a conduit, a warehouse for energy, a sensing device, a transmitter and a filtering system. Learning to bridge the split between mind and body, to access your own natural resources, is an exciting new educational process.

Inner resource management is the way to build a bridge between mind and body. To notice your instincts, innate knowledge and bodily responses and to use them in partnership with your rational capabilities will give you a full range of information, response and expression. The mind is a fine tool for discernment, application and action that collaborates with the wisdom of the heart and the direction of the gut. The wellness and vitality of the whole body as a living system reflects the wellness and vitality of its parts.

Learning to Manage Your Natural Resources

Here's a guide to some of your natural resources and how to use them.

Natural rhythm: your inner timeclock

Your pulse, the rhythm of your heart, beats in every cell of your body, telling you how fast or slow to go and when to go or stop. The pulse provides the pace that is right for you, an alternative to the rigid timeframes and schedules imposed from outside.

When I was in the corporate world, my daily timeframe was totally unnatural for me. Waking at 5:45 a.m., an ungodly early hour for my body, I would try desperately to get myself out of bed which would always take me until 6 a.m. Once up, I rushed around for an hour, getting ready for a long day that commenced with a 62-mile commute to work. Using evening hours for social activities, exercise and professional commitments, I rarely got home before 10 p.m., tired, stressed out and so wound up I couldn't sleep.

Over the last few years, I have followed my own natural rhythm more closely. As many mornings as possible, I let myself wake up when my body is ready. No more alarm clocks. I give myself 30 to 40 minutes before getting up for meditation. I allow myself to gently move into the day. Whether a Monday or Sunday, I tend to be raring to go by 8 a.m. My activities, work and social engagements are more carefully chosen. To minimize the number of things I do out of obligation, I ask myself, "What do you really want to do? What adds to your vitality? What nourishes you?" I go to sleep when I am tired, which tends to be between 11:30 p.m. and midnight.

Sometimes I wonder if I can trust my inner timeclock. "What if I have to wake up particularly early to give an important presentation? What if I'm traveling in a foreign country in a different time zone?" A voice inside of me recites a whole list of "what if's." When I am brave, I respond to the voice by saying, "Don't worry. I can wake up whenever I want to by simply programming myself before I go to sleep." When I'm scared or simply tired I might fall back on my old crutch, the alarm clock. However the more I take the risk of using my natural timeclock, the more evidence is given that I can trust my own natural sense of timing. If I listen to my own natural rhythm all day, every day, getting up in the morning is not a problem.

Chapter 4 included an exercise to help you find your natural rhythm. Here's an experiment you can try to become more familiar with your body rhythms:

On a weekend or when you have some time to yourself, let yourself go to sleep and wake up when your body is ready. If you are particularly worn out and depleted, you may find yourself going to bed particularly early and waking up particularly late. See if you can let your body choose your bedtime hour for several days. Notice what hour it tends to choose. Do you find a pattern emerging? What is your natural bedtime hour? See if you can let your body choose its waking hour for several days, and see what your natural waking hour is. Notice how you feel when you've chosen your sleeping time based on your inner timeclock. Is your thinking clearer? Your stress reduced? Do you feel more alert? Have more energy?

Your energy: the most fundamental resource

Energy is the most fundamental resource you have to manage. This is a resource to invest as well as a monitor of your overall health and well-being. How you live your life and care for your body affects your energy level. If you are not providing your body with sufficient rest, exercise, nourishment and quiet time, energy will be depleted. The more aware you are of your physical, emotional and spiritual needs, the better you can care for yourself and the more vital you can be.

The above experiment for discovering your natural sleep and waking time can also be used to become more familiar with your energy level. Do you have more energy when you follow your natural timeclock? Just by doing the experiment you may find yourself paying more attention to your energy level. Managing your energy involves knowing how you feel physically and emotionally, asking yourself what you need and taking care of yourself. As you become aware of your energy level, you can monitor it moment by moment. To become more aware of your energy level take a moment to notice: How are you feeling? Are you tired? Energized? Depleted? Full? Let yourself notice.

If you could let your body move into a position that reflects how you feel, what position would you be in? Would you slump? Sit erect? Lie down? Curl up? Move your shoulders back and forth? Become aware of how your body would want to move.

Try moving into that position now. How does it feel? Let yourself stay in the position until you feel complete. Very gently move out of the position into what now feels comfortable. Again notice your energy level. Has it changed?

To the degree that you learn to listen to your body, you can more fully experience and manage your energy level. For a steady supply of energy:

Become aware of your energy level. Do an energy check several times a day to notice how you are feeling and when your energy level changes.

Notice the relationship between your energy level and your feelings, both physical and emotional. Let yourself become familiar with how your body feels when you are sad, excited, bored and peaceful. Notice how your body would want to move in response to how you feel.

Let yourself pay more attention to what really matters to you. When you are doing things that you feel are important you tend to be more energized.

Give yourself time to rest and reflect. You need time to replenish and relax in your active life. A balance of rest and activity is necessary for a steady supply of energy.

Begin to notice how different foods affect your energy. Sugar and coffee may give you an initial charge, then leave you tired and edgy in a short time. Notice the difference between a food-induced high and a natural burst of energy that comes from being rested and taking care of yourself.

Exercise regularly. Exercise keeps you in touch with your body, releases tension and helps you stay energized.

The sources of wisdom within the body

While we all like to think of ourselves as "together, integrated people," inside each of us lives a cast of characters, each expressing their own opinion, experience and ideas. A child, a judge, a spirited warrior, a wise person and many others, male and female, young and old, live inside you. Have you noticed your mother's or father's voice giving advice? Is there a part of you that is hesitant and cautious and another part that is curious and adventurous? Perhaps you have a character, a judge, saying "That's not good enough," "You should have known better," or "Are you crazy?" The different characters are one of your natural resources, there to provide different points of view and to help you understand your wants and needs. Take a moment to list the different characters who live inside you and write down typical conversations.

Here are a few of my inner characters:

The judge: "That's not good enough, Linda." "Come on—do it right!"

The child: "I don't understand why people don't follow through on their commitments."

The artist: Draws, writes, dances, feels, expresses passion, inspiration and possibility.

The thinker: "Now, if you want to make this happen, you need to do the following things... ."

The wise one: Comes up with brilliant, often simple truths, organically and with great humility.

The angry adolescent: "You disappointed me so I'm going away!"

I've come to realize that each inner character knows a part of the whole truth. Two voices can argue and both be right. If you can learn to listen to the conversations, you can better understand how you are feeling and why, then choose a course of action that is truest to yourself.

Reaching Consensus: Head/Heart/Gut and Whole Self

As you try to make decisions, have you ever been ambivalent and regretted the way you acted? Often we act without finding out what is true to ourselves in a particular situation.

I love Carolyn Estes' definition of consensus, that "each one of us/part of us contains a piece of the whole truth."[1] When there is conflict, a part of the whole truth isn't yet expressed. When each piece of the whole truth is included, there is silence because there is nothing left to say.

The following technique enables you to consciously consult three different parts of yourself that collectively can help you see where you stand.

Exercise

Step 1: Choose a question you are wrestling with that you would like to have answered. It may be about something you want to do, something you want to know, or a decision you need to make. Examples: "Should I meet with Debbie on Thursday?" "What can I do about world hunger?" "What do I want for dinner?"

Step 2: Close your eyes and let yourself relax, giving yourself time and space to breathe. Whenever you feel ready, locate your physical heart. Let yourself become familiar with your heart, noticing how it feels. Ask your heart the question you have formulated. The heart may respond in silence. It may respond in words, feelings, images, physical sensations and/or colors. Let yourself notice whatever your heart has to say, however it responds.

Next, allow your focus to move to your gut. Where in your body does your gut live? Take a moment to notice its physical location and how it feels right now. When ready, ask your gut the question you have formulated and give the time and space for a response. Allow yourself to notice the response that may be similar or different from the heart's. Whatever you find is fine. There is no right or wrong reaction.

Now, allow your focus to shift to your head. Take a moment to notice where your head is located physically and how it feels. Whenever you are ready, ask your head the question you have formulated. Give your head the time and space to respond in its own way. Again, let yourself simply notice the response.

Then, allow yourself to review the responses of your heart, your gut and your head. Notice if they are similar or different, if they agree or disagree, if some are silent and others are talkative. Having reviewed the responses, ask your whole self the original question and see what your answer now is.

When ready, very slowly and gently, at your own pace, take a deep breath and bring your focus back into the room.

Step 3: On a piece of paper record what your heart said, what your gut said, what your head said and what your whole self said. Make some notes on what it was like to do this exercise. Was it comfortable? Uncomfortable? New? Familiar? What did you learn? How do you feel having asked the different parts for their opinions? How could you use this technique to help you live more true to yourself?

Here's a sample journal entry for a person doing this exercise:

Question Statement: "Should I call a friend to go out for dinner?"

Heart's Response: "I need company."

Gut's Response: "What if no one is available?"

Head's Response: "You've got too much work to do."

Whole Self's Response: "I want to and I'm afraid."

To bring the conversation to resolution, the person lets the heart, gut and head pursue a dialogue.

Heart: "I don't want to work tonight."

Head: "Yes, I know. I suppose I could come in early tomorrow morning."

Heart: "I bet Carol would go to dinner. She's spontaneous."

Gut: "Call Carol."

Whole Self: "I'll call Carol and ask her to go to dinner."

Chances are that you call upon your head, your heart and your gut to make choices and decisions every day. This exercise allows you to do so consciously. What are the different viewpoints each tends to take? I find my heart tells me what I really want, my gut reveals my intuitive answer, and my head explores the practical side of the matter at hand. Some experience the gut as the integrator, the mediator between heart and head. Or they experience the gut as the raw instinct, arriving intuitively at the same answer the head arrives at through careful thought.

Getting to Know the Body's Inner Landscape—The Body Scan

Having met with some of your inner characters, you can become more familiar with your body's inner landscape. The following technique, called a *body scan*, allows you to deepen awareness of your physical experience. While this technique is relaxing, most importantly it provides information about how you are currently feeling, why you are feeling this way and what you need to be more complete and vital.

The body scan works best if listened to on a tape or with a partner to guide you through. As you begin your journey inward, let your mind quiet and open. Allow your curiosity to lead you from moment to moment. Let yourself watch and observe what you are feeling and experiencing moment by moment, as though you were a photographer snapping pictures of all the nooks and crannies you discover as you move from place to place.

Try not to judge, understand or put meaning on what you find. Sometimes what you find is different than expected and might not make sense to the rational mind. Simply stay with your own experience, saying, "Isn't that interesting. ...That's curious. ..." You will find meaning emerges in time. You know what you need to know when you need to know it.

Preparation

The following is to be read as you prepare a tape of the exercise or by your partner if this exercise is being done with another person.

1. This exercise is designed to be done slowly and gently. Before starting the exercise, relax, let your mind quiet so that your voice becomes calm, soft and flowing. As you read the words printed below, imagine there is all the time in the world. See if you can read the exercise with love, patience and respect. The exercise is a kind of meditation.

2. During the exercise there will be a series of questions about how different parts of the body feel. These questions are meant to help focus attention on the body's terrain and aren't meant to be answered verbally. You should not give a verbal response to the questions.

3. You can't do this exercise "wrongly." Like a journey, a fishing trip or a walk through the woods, you never know exactly what you'll find when you set out. Be open to simply watching, noticing and discovering whatever is there. This becomes easier to do as you gain experience doing the exercise.

4. The words that appear in *italics* are ones that require inflection or emphasis as you read. Accentuate them slightly.

Exercise

Get comfortable, close your eyes, and give yourself space to breathe. Allow yourself to focus on your breath, coming in through your nose as you inhale, moving down your throat, filling your belly and bringing nourishment and support to the cells of your body. Let each cell take in just the amount needed in its own time and space. When each cell feels complete, let the nourishment and support provided be exhaled through the mouth, returning to the source. Have it return to you once again with your next inhalation as the circle of your breath completes itself. Take a moment to let yourself become more familiar with the circle of your breath.

Whenever you feel ready, take a moment to review what's happening in your life right now. How are you feeling about yourself? Your relationships with other people? Your work? Your home? Take a moment to review any parts of your life that seem important right now; see if any particular part of your life calls your attention more than any other. If it does, allow yourself to become more familiar with this part.

As you focus on this particular aspect of your life, let yourself notice some of the obstacles facing you. What limits are you bumping up against in yourself and others? What isn't the way you would like it to be? What don't you know or have? What seems to be missing? Let yourself become familiar with any obstacles, limits or missing pieces in this part of your life right now.

Whenever you feel ready, keeping your focus inside with your current experience, begin the body scan. Give yourself permission to just watch and notice whatever is happening, letting go for the moment of the need to analyze, judge or put meaning on your experience. Let the part of you that is curious lead the way. Allow your focus to begin with your head. Is it heavy? Light? Empty? Full? Talkative? Quiet? If there were a conversation in your head, what would it be? Take a moment to let yourself become more familiar with *whatever's* happening in your head *now*.

Now, allow your focus to shift downward to your neck and throat. How does it feel? Tight? Loose? Open? Closed? Safe? Vulnerable? Take a moment to become more aware of what is happening in your neck and throat *now*.

Allow your focus to shift downward to your heart. Notice what's happening there now. Is it tense? Relaxed? Present? Distant? Open? Closed? If there were a conversation in your heart, what would it be? Take a moment to become familiar with *whatever's* happening in your heart *now*.

Whenever you feel ready, allow your focus to shift to your solar plexus located at the bottom of your rib cage in the center of your body. What is happening there now. Is it solid? Delicate? Empty? Full? Connected? Separate? Take a moment to notice the sensations in your solar plexus *now*.

Next, allow your focus to shift even farther downward to the center of your belly. How does *it* feel? Is it tight? Loose? Open? Closed? Separate? Connected? If there were a conversation in your belly, what would that conversation be? Take a moment to become familiar with *anything* happening in your belly *now*.

When ready, continue downward to pelvis and genitals. Take a moment to notice what's happening there now. Are they energized? Depleted? Hungry? Full? Separate? Connected? Acquaint yourself with what is happening in your pelvis and genitals *now*.

Allow your focus to shift downward once again to your legs and tailbone. Notice what's happening there now. Are they heavy? Light? Energized? Depleted? Rooted? Uprooted? Take a moment to let yourself become more familiar with *whatever's* happening in your legs and tailbone *now*.

Whenever you feel ready, allow your focus to shift to all of your body. See if any one part calls your attention more than any other part. If one does, become familiar with it.

Now, at your own pace, slowly and gently take a deep breath and bring your focus back to the room.

As you open your eyes, take notes on what you found during the journey. Describe what you found in each part of your body in as much detail as you can. Pretend you are a photographer who took pictures. Record what you experienced. If you find yourself writing "It felt fine" or "It was okay," describe what "fine" or "okay" were like—for example, comfortable, warm, relaxed, distant....

Observations from the body scan

Your can organize your notes using the same format as this person who had just completed the body scan:

Area of life: Relationships

What's missing: Playmates, companions, people to have fun with.

Question: Why can't I find anyone to play with me?

Head: My head felt a bit tight and heavy, especially around the eyes. My eyes felt tight and tense, as though they were holding back tears. My mouth was tight, my jaw tense and my lips pushed together tightly. The conversation in my head was, "I'm scared. I don't want to do it all alone. I don't know what to do."

Neck and throat: My throat felt tight and constricted. It was hard for me to swallow and hard to breathe. My neck felt very vulnerable.

Heart: My heart felt a little heavy, especially toward the bottom, as though a weight were dragging it down toward my stomach, and yet it was pretty calm and peaceful. The conversation in my heart was, "I need to stop and relax. I need to let go."

Solar plexus: My solar plexus felt very tense and tight, like an iron wall. The outer layer of the solar plexus, from about 1" under the surface all the way to the skin, felt very thick. Underneath the wall I feel open and vulnerable. There's a quivering feeling inside the solar plexus there. I feel scared.

Center of the belly: I feel a knot that is very tight and heavy in the center of my belly. This knot is connected to a deep sadness in my heart. I feel a heavy sadness that can't express itself. It's stuck there. The conversation in my belly was, "Please, help me!"

Pelvis and genitals: I feel a tightness in my genitals, a holding on. I want to feel connected. My pelvis feels solid and linked to my tailbone.

Legs and tailbone: My tailbone feels strong, grounded, firmly rooted in the earth, yet a bit delicate. It feels particularly vulnerable on the back side, more strong and grounded toward the front and bottom. My legs feel two different ways: solidly rooted and soft, delicate. It's as though the little girl in me is the soft, delicate, scared part saying, "Please help me"; and the solid, rooted, grounded part is saying, "Everything's okay."

The part that called my attention most: The knot in the center of my belly. It goes deep into my very soul. My belly is scared; and my heart is praying, "Please God, this time, please."

What I learned from the body scan: I learned that I am both strong and fragile right now. I need to consider the scared, delicate part of me in setting my pace. I need to relax, to let go and to take it easy sometimes. I tend to keep working, doing, being active. Perhaps I am running away from myself through all my activity. I need to stop, lie down and be with my own fear. If I listen to my body I will stop running and take care of myself.

Focusing on areas that call your attention

Here is a technique that enables you to probe a part of your body that calls your attention. The technique is very much like "Getting to the Root of the Matter" introduced in Chapter 3. It is best done with closed eyes so you can focus your attention on the inner landscape rather than the details of the room around you.

Exercise

Step 1: Locate the physical area you wish to probe by doing a body scan or seeing where you feel tension, pain or anxiety in a particular part of your body.

Step 2: Become more familiar with the physical landscape of that part. How does the part you are working with feel physically? Is it tense, painful, numb? Exactly where is it located? Do you feel it on the inside or the outside? Does one particular point call your attention more than any other part? Place your hand on that place.[2]

Step 3: Ask the place that calls your attention most— where you have placed your hand—"What purpose are you serving?" See what words come to mind.

Step 4: Ask the same place, "And what matters about that?" or "And what's important about that?" Listen for the answer.

Step 5: Repeat the same question, "And what really matters about that?" as many times as you need to until you feel you are at the root of what really matters.

Step 6: Ask the part you've been working with, "Is there anything you need to know or hear or experience right now?" See what it says. If it needs to know something, answer it. If there are specific words needed, repeat them verbatim to the part. If physical contact is needed—being held, touched or caressed for example—give the part the kind of contact it needs (either visually in your mind, or physically).

Step 7: Continue to ask the part if it needs to know, hear or experience anything, responding by giving it what it asks for until finished.

When you feel complete, very slowly and gently take a deep breath, open your eyes and bring your focus back into the room. Take notes on what you learned.

Example of how this works

I have a tightness in my jaw. As I close my eyes, I feel my teeth clenching—that is where the tightness is focused. I feel the greatest pressure at the place where my upper teeth meet my lower teeth, especially toward the back of my mouth. I take my right hand and place it on my cheeks over the pressure point in my jaw. I close my fingers so they are as tightly clasped on my jaw as the pressure feels in the jaw itself. As I focus on the pressure between my teeth I feel sadness.

"What purpose are you serving?" I ask. "I'm scared," is the response, "I need something to hold onto." "What matters about that?" I then ask. "I don't want to be by myself," is the answer. "And what matters about that?" "I can't do it all alone. I can't take it anymore." I feel a sense of letting go in my heart and breathe a sigh of relief. The pressure in my jaw lightens. "Is there anything you need to know, hear or experience right now?" I ask the jaw. "You're okay," is the response. I then tell my jaw, "You're okay." Another sigh of relief. "Is there anything else you need to know or feel or experience right now?" I ask the jaw again. "I love you." I repeat the words "I love you." Again, a sigh of relief. "Is there anything else?" I ask again. "Tell me everything's going to be okay." So I do. Still another sigh of relief. "Is there anything else you need to know or feel or experience right now?" This time the answer is, "No."

I take a moment to notice how my jaw is feeling—lighter, more open, less tight. My heart feels full and light as well. I give myself enough space to breathe, take a deep breath and bring my focus back to the room. In my journal I write the details of the conversation and what I learned.

What happened: I felt a tightness in my jaw. As I closed my eyes I noticed this was particularly strong between my teeth. I felt a deep sadness as I focused my attention on the tightness. I felt scared—as though I were all alone, knew I couldn't do it all myself and that I was desperately trying to find something to hold on to. I needed to know I was okay, that I was loved and everything was going to be all right.

What I learned: I guess the little girl who lives inside me is still lonely. I need to take time to tell her she's okay, that I love her and that everything's going to be all right. Sometimes my fear moves me into action rather than reflection and self-care. Perhaps I can learn to notice my jaw's tightness more often, so I can relax and feel more secure.

Where Does Spirit Fit into the Picture?

Having acknowledged the place of the mind and learned to tap some of the wisdom of the body, you may be asking, "Where does the spirit fit in?" Just as mind cannot be separated from body, mind and body cannot be separated from spirit. I believe spirit lives inside each of us. One knows spirit through personal experience. I do not dare create a general definition of spirit, because I only know my own experience of its qualities. My spirit lives deep inside of me and, by its very nature, tests the limits of language.

Spirit is often confused with religion which is a structure, an institution, and/or a collection of rituals which grew out of a particular culture at a particular point in time for the pursuit and cultivation of spirit. Many of our religious traditions seem empty today, because over the years we have preserved the rituals and activities of the originating time and lost touch with how and why the rituals and activities were created. Often we confuse the rituals, practices and institutions with the spirit they were meant to honor and contain.

I encourage you to ask yourself where spirit fits into the picture for you and to create your own personal definition. In this light, I offer my own articulation of "What is spirit to me?"[2]

Spirit is a quality of inner feeling. My spirit is light and graceful—a dancer whose music is the fabric of life. It is the experience and expression of passion, vitality, energy—of being fully alive.

Spirit is a source of energy, inspiration, warmth and love. A fluid form of energy, it flows in me and through me. This energy reaches every cell with radiant, gentle light and radiates light from each cell out into the world. When the light of my spirit is shining within me and from me, my heart is warm and filled with love.

My spirit knows no bounds, no limitations. When I encumber my spirit, a part of me dies. Unburdened, it soars beyond the apparent limitations of the current moment, beyond my limitations as a human being and guides me to imagine what else might be possible.

My spirit knows what is true for me and my sense of purpose. Spirit is closely aligned with my heart. When my actions reflect what really matters, what is true for me, my spirit sings. Spirit is the voice of my soul. When I stray off my path, it cries and gently nudges me.

My spirit knows I have my own natural rhythm. It knows everything happens in the right time and place. Spirit is patient, even when I can't be. It knows each person living on this earth is a note in a symphony composed of many notes and melodies. Each note makes a unique sound when it is time. Together, the notes comprise a beautiful, multi-textured web of sound and feeling.

My spirit likes to dance, moving my body and expressing my heart. When spirit and body are united, I can move, run, sail and soar with grace and ease. If my body is the river bed, my spirit is the river—the gentle, warm currents that ripple, flow and weave from here to there. When heart and spirit are united, I am light, open, radiant, quiet and at peace.

Part III

Making
a
Difference

CHAPTER 8

Sustaining
Relationships

*People need to be known and seen for
who they are—as unique human beings.
Love comes out of the* SEEING *and the* KNOWING.
—ANN WEISER
DIRECTOR, ACTION LINKAGE

Everything that happens in the world happens through relationships. Whenever two people come together, even for a
moment, they exchange looks, feelings, thoughts, ideas and
energy. In the mirror of another person we see ourselves more
clearly—our gifts and our limits, our desires and our needs.

While everyone needs to love and be loved, thinking people
often find themselves clumsy at relating. Our relationships
involve many trade-offs: between my needs and yours, between my intimacy with you and my sense of self, between my
primary relationship with one person and my relationships
with other people.

As thinking people we view relationship as an "object" or a
"thing"—something one either has or gets, rather than something to be co-created and lived moment by moment with
another person. So many people say, "I want a relationship"
and mean a single, intimate, love relationship with a sexual
partner. In this light, friendships are different from relationships and are instead used to describe what relationships
become when they "aren't working."

This thinking has restricted the quality and kinds of relationships we engage in. We live with many images and rules about how relationships are supposed to be rather than being open to discover how they can be. A conscious/compassionate person strives to create *sustainable relationships*—ones that nourish and enrich both people involved, extend to all aspects of our lives, have the strength and flexibility to endure and evolve over time, and provide a path to personal growth and service.

Every relationship is unique as are the individuals who comprise each relationship. Wholeness is a key to sustainable relationships: Each person brings all parts of the self to the party and creates a space where all parts of oneself and the other can be seen, understood and affirmed.

What is needed to create a sustainable relationship? How can you live with vision in relation to another person?

The Dance of Relationship

The best image I have for relationship is the dance. In essence, life is a dance and all of us are dancers. In relationships we are repeatedly coming together and moving apart, with periods of connection and times of separation. When we come together, we see and are seen, touch and are touched, feel fuller and more complete in our connection. Through being with another we become more wholly ourselves.

The foundation for healthy relationships with others is a healthy relationship with oneself. If you come to another person full, you are energized and sustained. If you come to another empty, while the connection may feel ecstatic any separation will be devastating and painful. When you are not in touch with your own wholeness and look to another for completion, your relationships are stressed. Before you can dance with a partner you need to be able to dance by yourself. You need to feel the rhythm of the music, hear how it inspires you to move and learn your unique style of movement and expression. Just as you have your own natural rhythm, each relationship with another has its own natural rhythm.

Relationship as a Living Organism

When you meet someone with whom you feel an immediate rapport, questions you might ask are: "What will this relationship become?" "Will we be friends or lovers?" "Will we be colleagues or associates?" "Will this person stay or go?" You may tend to focus your attention right away on the form the union will take not even considering that a new relationship is like an embryo that requires time, care and attention to grow into whatever may evolve.

At the beginning of any relation there's so much you don't know. To feel the spark of connection with another person is both exciting and terrifying. There are three characters to become acquainted with: *me*, *you* and *we*. The needs of all three must be understood, considered and attended to for the relationship to thrive. Many tend to rush too quickly into defining the identity of the young organism that is just emerging and developing. Well-intentioned efforts to understand and shape a relationship can actually smother the seedling if those efforts come from fear of the intangible and the unknown.

Relationships flourish in a framework, a container, that provides the degree of structure needed to support the organism's growth and development over time. It takes time and energy to get to know each other, learning to communicate, understanding visions and values, and working with differences. If you focus too much on form or structure, you may limit and suffocate the relationship; if you pay too little attention, it may collapse from lack of support.

Trust

The key building block for sustainable relationships is trust. Trust is a bond that evolves as two persons get to know one another and experience safety in opening their hearts to each other. Trust develops when you respect one another's needs and develop a history of common experience and caring.

Intimacy

Intimacy is something everyone craves and yearns for. It measures the depth and quality of relating and is the very food of sustainable relationships. Intimacy can encompass the physical, emotional and spiritual. Many in our culture limit intimacy to the sexual bond. While intimacy can be present in sexual relations, it comes from relating heart to heart. In this sense, you can be intimate with many people without sexuality. Intimacy can connect you deeply with people in different ways.

Intimacy nourishes people in a very fundamental way, enabling us to thrive and grow. While everyone craves this, most of us also are scared of true intimacy. When you are intimate, you are vulnerable and exposed as you let yourself be seen and known by another person. Your defenses are down, and your soft underbelly, who you really are, is exposed. While you need to be vulnerable in order to connect with another person at a profound, deep and sacred level, such an experience is risky.

"I have trouble connecting with my vision and I have trouble being intimate," one workshop participant confided. "Can there be any relationship between the two?" "What happens when I ask you to find and connect with your heart?" I asked in response. "Not much," was her reply. "I don't find much of anything there." Her heart was distant, perhaps even hiding. Having been wounded deeply as a child and an adult, she had to protect herself from being hurt again. Both intimacy and vision come from the heart. Your heart needs to feel safe in order to experience either.

A good way to begin to cultivate intimacy in your life is to learn to be intimate with yourself. The voices of your harshest critic and your most loving supporter both live inside you. You must learn to know and dance with both in order to relate fully with another person. What is your critic trying to tell you? If it could give you the same message lovingly rather than judgmentally, what would it say? My critic often tells me I'm not good enough, and no matter how hard I try, I should try even harder. When I see my critic from a loving place, she is really saying, "I want to do a good job. I want to do the best I can." The loving voice seeks to pamper me and see that I'm good to myself. "Get yourself a bunch of flowers—the most beautiful ones you can find. Get a massage. Lie in your backyard in the sun." I feel happy when I oblige.

Being intimate requires a lot of inner strength, including knowing your personal boundaries. Boundaries help you determine: Where do I end and where do you begin? How much space do I need to be close to another without losing a sense of myself? What are my needs and what are my limits?

Boundaries enable you to organize and orchestrate your individual energy and your joint energy. They are both a protection and a gateway. Boundaries keep you safe and, when it's time to relate, allow you to be open, to give and receive. If boundaries are too rigid you have no space to breathe. If they are not defined enough you will find connection or relationship hard.

I learned a lot about boundaries and relating as I came to know a friend who was remarkably like me. Our personal and professional interests were much the same, as were our aspirations. Our inner children could play together at home, on the town or in the woods, and our purposeful adults could talk about travel, healing and the future of mankind. As we were drawn closer we'd reach a point where my friend would start pushing me away. Our space for relating would disappear and so would my friend. I'd feel lost and confused; yet I hung on, not wanting to let go. "What's going on?" I would wonder.

This friend finally told me a story that provided insight. Once upon a time there was a wise king who met a wise and powerful woman. He was drawn to her, yet always resisted. One day as he let himself succumb and embrace her, he found himself shrinking in her arms. First he became a younger man. Then he became a boy, then a younger boy, and an infant, and finally nothing at all. He disappeared. All that was left was the woman holding the crown in her arms.

"You and I are very much alike," my friend said. "We both want the same things so much, and yet as I get close to you I'm afraid I'll disappear. I can't risk that; I need to get stronger in myself before I can relate to you." While hearing this was painful, I knew it was true. My friend was pushing me away so he wouldn't disappear. Until you are anchored in yourself, it's hard to relate to someone else.

Conflict

While conflict is a word that makes many cringe, it is a natural part of relating to others. While we often fear it, conflict in itself is not dangerous but is part of the process of coming together, getting close, and building trust and intimacy. By confronting us with our blindspots and growing edges, conflict forces us to open and grow.

Danaan Parry, a lecturer on conflict resolution, describes seven points for understanding and resolving conflict:[1]

1. Conflict is like breathing. There is no relationship without it.

2. The presenting problem is almost never the real problem. Getting stuck in the former isolates you from yourself and others and prevents resolution.

3. To resolve conflict, you need to create a safe space. A safe space is one in which you feel free to share your vulnerabilities, knowing that you won't be judged, attacked or reacted to.

4. Conflict is about intimacy. To be intimate requires doing something that will get attention. Being human, we tend to create some kind of negativity in order to be noticed. The core of real connection is shared pain.

5. Change occurs right at the edge of your comfort zone. Our comfort zone is a place we go to heal, to relax, to be quiet. We need to step out beyond that zone to grow and to learn.

6. That which you resist persists. Conflict seeks resolution, just as a discordant note in a melody seeks resolution. Sooner or later, you need to get to the root of the matter at hand.

7. You need to be 100% present in a conflict. This means you are not only physically, but also emotionally and mentally present. The more open you can be to your feelings, to what is happening around you, your responses and reactions, the more genuinely you can participate in the conflict at hand. Being present also involves letting go of preconceived images, outcomes, and judgments, viewing and receiving whatever is happening here and now with a fresh set of eyes and an open heart.

Partnership

Partnership, as used here, is a quality of relating that can be developed in many kinds of relationships. It is an attitude toward relationship that is based on respect, mutuality and balance. For me, partnership implies a commitment to work on a relationship in a way that nourishes both individuals and the partnership as a whole.

Partnership enables people to come together and be received as whole, complete and unique individuals with strengths and weaknesses, gifts and limitations. Partners relate from a deeper level than personality or ego, call it the true self or the soul. At this level, what on the surface may seem insurmountable differences give way to common core values. Differences allow for complementarity, while common core values and a common vision provide a foundation and direction for the relationship to grow. Each partner brings 100% of themselves to the relationship and assumes 100% responsibility for the successful growth and evolution of the partnership. To sustain a partnership involves care and attention to self and the partnership. Partnership is a way of relating fully with another person.

Partnership comes in different forms—marriage, business and life. The following three partnerships illustrate what living in this quality of relationship means.

Purpose and service

While healthy relationships nourish and support the individuals who comprise them, they also serve a purpose beyond personal growth and fulfillment alone. The common values and vision that bring people together and sustain relationships provide the foundation for defining a common purpose for the relationship.

I believe human beings by nature want to contribute to a better world. When we are loved and whole, as in a healthy relationship, wanting to spread that love and energy is natural. To give our gift in collaboration with another person is both invigorating and exciting. Relationship, in this sense, becomes an incubator for service to others and, ultimately, to all life.

John-Richard Turner, 54, and Troye Groot, 40, psychotherapists, and co-directors of the Institute for Whole Self Therapy, share a common purpose and commitment to global service. They met at a conference in Swanick, England, in 1984. Their work, "Whole Self Therapy," recognizes that it is possible to trace many experiences in a person's emotional/mental composition to their gestation, including the pre-natal and peri-natal period.[4]

Troye realized quite soon after they met that they each were working to accomplish the same vision. Her first reaction was terror, to run away. To acknowledge that she and John-Richard had work to do together would mean a drastic change in lifestyle for Troye. She was used to a comfortable private life in Amsterdam. John-Richard's work took him around the world. Two years after their meeting, John-Richard and Troye embraced the common work they had to do and became partners in life and work. In 1987 they visited 13 countries, seeing individual clients, giving workshops and talks, and working actively in the Association for Prenatal and Perinatal Psychology of North America and the International Society for Prenatal Psychology. Their common mission is "to bring to human awareness the importance of conscious conception, conscious pregnancy, conscious birthing and conscious child-growing." John-Richard comments:

> Having acted the vision alone for 15 years, sharing the vision in partnership is the most wonderful thing I can imagine. Working toward a vision in partnership feels like being completed. The relationship becomes a vehicle or a container for living out our vision. Only since I've met Troye have I been able to stop asking the question, "Is this work my purpose for being in the world?"
>
> When you live alone, blind spots can emerge and be pushed aside. When you are working together, blind spots emerge constantly and must be worked at. In a difference of opinion or dispute, we are both totally open to discussing the issue and bringing understanding to what happened so we don't dwell on it. Key elements are mutual respect, responsibility and a sense of process.

Even once they had accepted their mutuality of vision and purpose, John-Richard and Troye faced challenges. Troye, who is Dutch, had to learn to work in English, a language foreign to her. She had to learn to do her work in a different way and to change the structure of her life. Her lifestyle changed from one of being alone in a familiar place to one of constant change and travel. John-Richard had to learn how to take Troye into consideration when making decisions. "I need to be able to explain why things have to be done in a certain way without being controlling."

While their different backgrounds and different styles presented challenges, the benefit has been a kind of synergy. John-Richard handles the marketing and sales part of the work, since he likes contacting people and setting schedules. Troye handles the finance and administration, as she enjoys managing the organizational aspects, making sure all the details are taken care of.

Dumont, Moriarty & Associates

Dumont, Moriarty & Associates is a small business—in their own words, "a placement firm specializing in managerial, professional, administrative, secretarial and office support positions; contract personnel; and training and development specialists." Located in Boston, the company started out over eight years ago as the creation of three initial partners, one woman and two men, who had been long-term friends. Its evolution has led it through many different phases—including expansion of personnel and services, a change of name, and even the departure two years ago of one of the founding partners. What has characterized the firm through all the different phases, including the departure of an original partner, is a full commitment to partnership. Rickie Moriarty says:

> People have to go into the partnership with a high level of trust, commitment, flexibility and an even temperament. We never brought our personal baggage into the business, yet we accommodated one another's needs. If someone had something going on—a vacation, a college reunion—we always covered for them. There was an absence of pettiness. We worked as a team. If someone had a bad season, the others would boost them up.
>
> There is a real sense of camaraderie among the partners, a common effort to keep the spirit alive. Six months into the business, one of the partners came down with hepatitis. We paid his family his full salary for the entire eight weeks he was sick. We had a high level of commitment to one another.

Even though the business was young and vulnerable, the partners put relationship first. "Often partners don't look at the long haul." These partners certainly did.

Rickie's advice to people going into a partnership:

1. Do the things you do well, not those you don't.

2. Be selective. Know your own limitations. Don't spread yourself too thin (yet everyone does).

3. Be willing to give that extra bit. This includes time, energy, and sometimes doing things you don't like to do.

In a partnership, power is something each person brings to the relationship and cultivates in the other. Power comes from feeling whole in oneself, in knowing one's strengths and limitations, and appreciating the complementary qualities another person brings to the partnership.

The UV Family

The UV Family is a core group of four individuals, one man and three women, who have lived and worked together in true partnership for over 20 years. Joe Dominguez, Vicki Robin, Monica Wood and Evy McDonald live in Seattle, Washington, and have traveled throughout the United States in a custom-designed motor home conducting seminars and serving humanity in a variety of ways. Once a financial consultant on Wall Street, Joe, having achieved financial independence at age 30, retired and shifted his focus from "success *in* the world" to "success *of* the world." [2] Monica met Joe on Wall Street where she worked as his assistant. Vicki's background includes acting and film production. Evy, a nurse, directed an intensive coronary care unit in Arizona. Together they have founded the New Road Map Foundation dedicated to personal and planetary healing. They talked to me about their partnership:

> Our origins span from a Nebraska turkey farm to New York City's Spanish Harlem, from Catholic through Methodist to Jewish. ...The only things we had in common when we came together were inquiring minds, willingness to risk and a dogged perseverance in our search for truth. We are clearly a mongrel breed. We are not "soul mates." We were not "made for each other." At the same time, we have consciously learned to be for each other and for the world, and in this sense we do feel that how we see and how we "do" our relationship can be a blueprint for others.
>
> Intent on reaching truth, we found that the first door we needed to go through was honesty—absolute honesty. With each other we committed to living unedited lives—to show-

ing all the shots, even the "out takes" that normally end up on the cutting room floor. Since fear of the consequences was the biggest barrier to truth, we established some rules and rituals for a safe space to communicate—where each person shared their thoughts and feelings until they felt complete, while the others listened carefully with no judgment, no interruption and no feedback. These "heart sharings" allowed us to train ourselves to be truthtellers.

When we listened without judgment and shared without editing, we found that we were constantly in love with each other. It wasn't love as we had known it—love as a reaction to another person. It was love that came simply from removing all the resistance to each other....Love wasn't an emotion (though wonderful emotions went along with it), and it wasn't a response; it was more like a choice. Love was a space. It couldn't be given or received, only entered.

Personal responsibility and commitment are key elements in the partnership among the members of the UV Family.

10 Qualities Needed for Sustaining Relationship

From my own experience and from the experiences shared by others, certain qualities emerge as necessary for the care and feeding of a sustainable relationship. You need to cultivate these in yourself before you can give them to another person. The more completely you can love yourself, becoming familiar with the nooks and crannies and with your own wholeness, the more open you can be with other people and the more you can love them for who they truly are.

Honesty and truth

Be true to yourself, own your own truth and communicate this to others. Everyone aspires to do this. To risk being naked with yourself and with others, to find out what this means to each of us, takes time and experience.

Fullness

So often we feel we have to change or give up a piece of ourselves in order to be loved by another. We may need to grow; we don't need to give up something essential or precious. One can sacrifice self both by sharing too much and by witholding too much. We have most to give when we accept and love ourselves first.

Seeing the whole picture

Own the wholeness in self, others and the situation at hand. Some of us tend to focus either only on the good or on what's wrong. In relating you need to develop total vision to see everything that is there; this includes the current reality and the possibility, the joy and the pain. In time you learn that while the truth may be painful, not knowing the truth is even more painful.

Acting from the heart

So often in relating we act from our heads. We censor, reject or deny our hearts to protect ourselves from being vulnerable, from getting hurt. Relating from the heart takes great courage, yet is essential for the growth and development of a vital relationship.

Presence: being there and caring

I never cease to be amazed at how much healing comes from just being there for someone, being present and caring. "Being there" means being open and present mentally, emotionally, physically, and spiritually—seeing and receiving who the other person really is without judgment. Presence allows someone to reveal vulnerabilities, innermost thoughts and feelings. Being there becomes a privilege, sharing another's pain, joy and life experience is one of the greatest gifts one can receive.

Sharing yourself

The more you share of yourself, the more you open yourself to others, the safer you make it for them to share themselves and be open with you. You begin by owning your own vulnerability and becoming more intimate with yourself. Taking risks in sharing feelings, dreams, concerns and experiences with another deepens and enriches the relationship, enabling both to be more fully present in the relationship.

Choosing to learn and grow

Relationship with another is a rich opportunity for personal growth. Because other people serve as mirrors, they help us see parts of ourselves that we might miss alone. As we grow, we nourish the relationship and allow both the other person and the relationship to grow as well.

Commitment

Making a commitment to self and to the relationship means you both agree to find a way to make things work for each and for the relationship as a whole. Relationships, like all living organisms, need time, care and attention in order to live and to grow. Commitment provides the safety needed to work through conflict.

Common values and a common vision

Common values provide the foundation for relating, showing us how we are alike, and validating what really matters to us. A common vision provides a common purpose and a sense of direction for the relationship's growth.

Lightness, humor and play

For anything to be sustained, you need enjoyment. While we often relate as serious, purposeful adults, our inner child knows what we love and care about, what nourishes our spirits and our hearts.

The Spiral of Relationship

I'm strong...I'm weak
I'm soft...I'm hard
I'm full...I'm empty
I'm everything...I'm nothing
I can dance to every note you beat on your drum
And I can fall on my face gracelessly
My heart venturing forward
Worst foot forward
Best foot forward
Which is which?
It's hard to tell
In the pot all melts together
Vegetable soup
Simmering in the heat of passion
In the heart of passion

Getting better over time
Deepening and thickening with a
full range of experience
Together and apart
Connected and alone
Inside and out
And round about
The dance of life
An embryo becoming a body
To hold what will be
Que será, será
What will be, will be.[4]

Relationship Mandala:
Looking at the Whole Picture

The following exercise can be used to see all the aspects of a relationship including the common values/vision/point of connection, the reality of what the relationship is right now and the possibility of what it might become. This exercise can be done by partners in a relationship—individually or jointly.

You will be constructing a relationship mandala, a circular drawing that allows you to illustrate parts of the relationship and the relationship as a whole.

Preparation

On a piece of paper, draw a large circle. Divide and label it as in Diagram 8:1 on the next page.

Exercise

Step 1: *Identify common values, common vision, points of connection.* Answer the following questions:
- What values do we share?
- What is it we both want right now?
- What is it we both want for the future?
- What is essential to both of us?
- What is it we have in common?
- What do we both care about greatly?

Now, in the center of the circle draw images and write down the common values, vision and points of connection that provide the core of the relationship.

RELATIONSHIP MANDALA

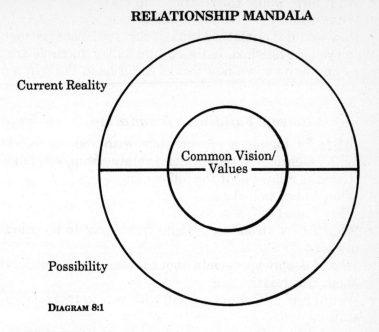

DIAGRAM 8:1

Step 2: *Looking at the current reality.* Answer the following questions:

- What's working?
- What isn't working?
- What is the form of the relationship?
- What does each person want from the relationship?
- Where are differences?
- What are joint accomplishments?
- What are limitations?
- What do you appreciate or value about the other person?
- How well does the relationship meet your needs?

Now, in the top half of the circle draw images and write down how things currently are in the relationship. (You may want to divide the half circle to include the dark side and the light side of current reality.)

Step 3: *Looking at the possibility.* Answer these questions:

- If the relationship could be any way you wanted it to be, how would it be?
- What would be different from the way things are right now?

- What form would the relationship take?
- What would you give to the relationship?
- How would the relationship nourish you? Your partner?

When you are finished, in the bottom half of the circle draw images and write down how things *could* be in the relationship.

Exercise followup: building a foundation

As a basis for having a conversation with your partner(s) about the essentials of sustaining a relationship, you might want to make notes about the following:

- What I need to feel safe.
- What I need to feel seen.
- What I need (from myself and from you) to be true to myself.
- What I deeply appreciate about myself, about you, and about this relationship.
- What I find difficult in myself, with you, in this relationship.
- How I want this relationship to be in my heart of hearts.
- How I would describe the quality of relating I want us to have.

You can then talk together about each of the items and jointly determine how you need to build the relationship that works for you.

CHAPTER 9

Humanizing Organizations

*Organizations lie midway along the line between
the individual and the collective.
They take from both and give to both.
My belief is that an organization, to be truly organic
(and thus creative), must be able to fuse together the masculine
and feminine elements of its potential.*

— *FRANCIS KINSMAN*
ONE EARTH MAGAZINE

All of us live in organizations, whether a company, a family,
a community or a network. What brings us together in an
organization is a common interest or a common purpose,
sometimes practical, sometimes lofty. Because so many of us
spend so much of our time in the workplace, this chapter will
focus on the organizations where we work.

Many of the organizations we work in exist to make a profit.
While profit is necessary for the growth, care and feeding of a
healthy organization, a conscious/compassionate organization also focuses on other values and ideals. The conscious/
compassionate organization exists to provide a service, acts as
a channel through which resources flow from the world back
to the world, and carefully manages these resources.

An organization enables people to come together and take
common action. In this sense it is a vehicle—allowing each of
us to go further than we could alone. Likewise, the organization is a bridge that extends our reach beyond our own limits
into the world at large. The organization is a place where we
can lead, where we can learn, and where we can act on our
convictions in collaboration with others. Through conscious/

compassionate organizations, we are nourished in order to nourish others and our common home, the Earth.

As we as human beings evolve from adolescence to maturity, we need to rethink the purpose and structure of our organizations. The organizations we have created as thinking humans are mechanistic. Many of these models grew out of the industrial age and focus on quantifying and differentiating, separating pieces from the whole. Profit has been separated from service, good business sense from basic human values, short-term goals from long-term needs, individual success from collective destiny. Competition, autonomy, planning and control all have merits. Yet each perpetuates separation of individuals, communities and nations from one another and from our natural resources.

Our view of organizations needs to expand so that we can see them as the living systems, the organisms, they actually are. Organizations are comprised of people, living organisms, who contribute to the organization's well-being and in turn are sustained by it. The interrelationship of people, organization and environment cannot be ignored. One's health and well-being are dependent on others. Indeed the organization is a body, and the principles related to the care and feeding of an organization are much the same as those for individuals. Every organization's mind, body and spirit need to be attended to in order to sustain and keep it vital.

Evolving from Mechanistic to Organic Organizations: Gaean Economics

The word economics is derived from the Greek *oikos* which means household. In the twentieth century our household is the planet. The Greek word *Gaea* is the name of the great Earth goddess, mother of all, creator of creators. In time Gaea has come to mean the earth herself as a living organism.

Gaean economics[1] goes back to these roots and refers to a shift that goes beyond concern for individual businesses or organizations to the Earth's economy. It is a sustainable model derived from nature providing practical means to integrate the way we live our lives, conduct our business, invest our money and interact with one another in our common household. Understanding Gaean economics will help us create and manage organizations for our next evolutionary phase. The Gaean framework will be used here to explain the difference between mechanistic and organic organizations.

Traditional models of business illustrate how a mechanistic organization operates. The current business world is based on four principles: 1) profit maximization—getting the most financial return on the resources you invest; 2) competition—survival of the fittest, creating winners and losers in the marketplace; 3) scarcity and limitation—there are not enough time, money, people or materials; good management achieves goals within the confines of limited resources; and 4) short-term orientation—accountability and success are judged each quarter, longer-term possibilities and implications of today's actions are ignored. These principles contain trade-offs which in fact foster loss, depletion and separation.

Comparing a Gaean and a Mechanistic Organization

There are many points of distinction between a Gaean or organic organization and a mechanistic one. In comparing and contrasting the two approaches, I do not intend to position them as polarities. Many practical methods of traditional business are fundamental to the successful operation of any organization. Yet we tend to forget that methods are tools and not answers. We often ignore the qualitative aspects of the organization. The mechanistic model focuses on the masculine aspects of organization, while the Gaean model includes the feminine and organic as well as mechanistic elements. Balancing goal and context, result and process, long term and short term is the art of conscious/compassionate management.

How the world is viewed

Our understanding of the nature of life provides the underlying structure for our institutions. The belief that life evolved through competition and survival of the fittest is reflected in our economy and world political system. Both the life sciences and the workplace are teaching us that nature does not work

DIAGRAM 9:1

Comparing Mechanistic and Gaean Organizations

DIMENSION	MECHANISTIC	GAEAN
How the world is viewed	Competition—survival of the fittest	Community—symbiosis
How creation/innovation takes place	Alone/individualism	With others/collaboration/co-creation
How organizations are managed	Planning and control—making things happen	Natural rhythm—balancing action and letting go
The basis for hiring	Skills and techniques	Personal purpose, vision and unique gifts
How the organization relates to the environment	Unconsciousness—exploitation, depletion	Consciousness, respect, consideration
The context	Narrow: the industry	Broad: the earth
How time is viewed	Now and the next quarter	Now in the context of the long term
Primary resource managed	Money	Energy
The role money plays	An end—the means of keeping score	A means—one of several resources
Who is accountable	Shareholders	Stakeholders

in an exclusive *either/or* manner, but rather in an inclusive *both/and* manner.

These new understandings of the conscious/compassionate stage provide an alternative model for our world institutions. Competition can be a tiring and depleting pursuit. Much energy is expended in the process of trying to survive, and losing is often the result. The question becomes: To what end are we competing? While a positive by-product of competition is more attention to quality and the needs of the marketplace, the underlying motivation is often fear. Many good opportunities are never discusssed or pursued for fear of "losing."

In contrast, more symbiotic relationships would allow room for all good ideas in the world of business. If we recognize the natural interconnections and interdependencies within and between organizations, we realize the value of managing organizations cooperatively. This creates continuity and a flow or exchange of energy. We recognize our efforts are part of something that is larger than we are. Each organization, each idea, each product comprises one part of a larger whole. Every idea has its place and time.

How creation/innovation takes place

The familiar profile of the entrepreneur suggests a lone individual as the model of success, framed only in the context of an isolated quest. The individual is not seen as part of a larger whole nor is the organization seen as a vehicle for serving the world as well as the individual. Entrepreneurial organizations typically have embodied and institutionalized the personality of their founders.

A collaborative/co-creative approach to innovation acknowledges that no one has to do it all alone. Doing it alone is unnatural. Each person has special talents and shortcomings. We are at our best when we do what we love and what comes naturally. When we do what we don't like because we think we have to, we are weak. Adding the strengths and talents of others to our own when building an organization provides flexibility and depth. A conscious/compassionate entrepreneur builds an organization as a forum for common vision and collaboration, enhancing the possibilities for success and for a positive social impact.

How organizations are managed

The institution of business today is based on mind over matter, making things happen and being in control. This reflects our thinking stage of development—separating the head from the rest of the body, viewing humanity as the dominant or superior species on the planet, and believing that force needs to be exerted to make things work.

Organizations built upon these premises eschew the reality of nature and life. Life offers a fundamental structure, a natural rhythm we can use to guide us that is less exhausting.

In nature, periods of quiet, stillness or dormancy are followed by periods of creation, blossoming and renewal. Business cycles, by comparison, don't recognize that individuals have their own cycles or rhythms. Today organizations are so action-oriented that the quiet, reflective, creative time necessary to replenish our resources and revitalize ourselves is not valued or allowed.

By choosing to ignore living matter and natural cycles, we limit our potential. We fail to access many resources by separating the mind from the body. As we learn to balance active and reflective time, discover our own rhythms and those of our organizations, our actions can become synchronized with the rhythms of other people, organizations and life.

The basis for hiring

Employees in organizations today are seen as resources, attributes, and skills, hired for what they can *do*, not for who they *are*. Organizations are carefully engineered machines and a person's skills represent a part needed for the machine to operate. Value is determined by external characteristics more than internal qualities. This approach is geared to mechanistic efficiency and lacks the creativity of a living organism.

A Gaean organization acknowledges that spirit, heart and soul—as well as the practical, operational and material elements—are fundamental to vital management. The Gaean organization looks at employees not as parts but as people with special gifts and talents, who bring a sense of personal purpose to the organization's purpose, along with aspirations that can be integrated into the organization's needs. When these dimensions are recognized as essential in the employment process, the result is a richer, more spirited organization made up of a network of creative resourceful individuals.

How the organization relates to the environment

The profit-maximizing philosophy underlying traditional business practice says "get the most out of the least." *The most* is defined in financial terms—with productivity, business, and innovation all being translated into money. Over-emphasizing dollars can result in exploitation of people and the

Earth. The mechanistic organization sees the environment as a source of resources or inputs from which to derive maximum output without considering the impact that resource extraction has on the Earth's health, well-being and sustainability.

The Gaean organization recognizes that nature is indeed abundant in resources but that her bounty needs to be cared for, respected and replenished. The Gaean organization also considers the impact these economic processes and by-products have on the environment. Undergirding such an organization is a profit-optimizing philosophy—to seek a level of profit that considers, respects and sustains all "stakeholders," i.e., the stockholders, customers, employees, suppliers, the Earth and all those who have a vested interest in its operation and final products.

The context

In mechanistic organizations the focus is on dates, events and facts. Such a perspective may move things quickly and in a logical fashion but often limits seeing the organization's global or wholistic effects. In this sense the organization is not seen in context; the largest frame of reference is usually limited to industry or class.

The Gaean organization recognizes that an organization is essentially a vehicle connecting person and planet. An organization can have a profound impact on the world—positively or negatively. The Gaean organization recognizes that life is a web of living systems. Larger organisms are built from many smaller ones. We need to see the whole to understand the actual roles and meanings of the parts.

How time is viewed

Mechanistic organizations, particularly businesses, live with a continuous sense of urgency. The pace is fast. The traditional manager must achieve results *now*. The pressure, immediate and short-term, makes looking at the bigger picture difficult.

The Gaean organization recognizes that opportunity exists in each moment but that each moment is part of a larger time context. There is a natural rhythm to a business life cycle, and the art of management is to move with the moment while keeping longer-term goals and objectives in mind. This relationship to time is more of connection than pursuit.

Attitude toward money

In the mechanistic organization, *money* is the measure of success, the fundamental criterion for making decisions, the bottom line, the way of keeping score. The value of other resources such as time, human energy and materials are determined solely in terms of money.

The Gaean organization emphasizes the management of *energy*, recognizing that materials are energy packages, that human beings contribute different types of energy and that money is actually a measurement of the exchange of energy. Small businesses will often substitute time and energy for money as they are developing. Other costs in addition to monetary ones are considered as well. The health of people and the environment, for example, receive high priority in the Gaean organization because people need to be healthy to be productive.

While money is managed as one of many resources in the Gaean organization, it is a means rather than an end. Money is seen as the life blood which allows for the growth, care and feeding of the organization and the people who comprise it.

Who is accountable

Mechanistic organizations are accountable to a small constituency. In public corporations the constituents are the stockholders. In exchange for financial investment, stockholders own pieces of the business. The Gaean organization is accountable to a much larger constituency: all the people and environments that relate to, provide resources for and affect the organization.

A Gaean organization's constituents are stakeholders. A successful Gaean organization must respect this broader constituency. This implies that a new set of values needs to be applied to goal-setting and performance evaluation. The Gaean organization recognizes the interconnection and interdependency of various constituents all of which need to be considered for sustainability.

Organizations Which Are Managed as if People and the Earth Really Mattered

The Gaean philosophy may seem far removed from the world of work as most of us know it. I have been delighted, however, to discover that this philosophy is a reality for a growing number of businesses that are successful by both traditional and conscious/compassionate standards. The Body Shop, Co-op America and Bread & Circus are three organizations which use a commitment to people, society and the Earth that is as striking as their ability to operate successfully in the marketplace. Two are for-profit corporations, one a nonprofit. One is based in London, two in the United States. All have international networks, whether for sourcing or distributing their products. All understand the necessity of profit and the importance of long-term vision; all feel a responsibility to their many stakeholders and to the place of people, purpose and values in an organization.

The Body Shop: understanding the responsibility of profit

The Body Shop, an internationally successful cosmetic company based in London, is as bold and adventurous as its founder, Anita Roddick. The child of Italian immigrants, Anita first applied her theatrical flair to teaching then secured a job with the United Nations and traveled around the world. In her travels to North Africa, India, Australia, South America and Polynesia, she particularly noticed the local women's skin. "In those hot places it should have been dry and cracked, but it was like satin."[2] She discovered that the secret was in natural products including cocoa butter, mud and aloe—the juice of the cactus leaf.

Tired of the long hours involved in running a successful business with her husband Gordon, Anita decided "to do something more regular, like open a shop."[3] She started 12 years ago with no money; today she boasts 110 shops around the world.

Her first shop in Brighton, England, was located between two funeral parlors. "They sent me a solicitor's letter saying I couldn't call this shop 'The Body Shop'."[4] Anita turned adversity into opportunity and through a phone call to the local newspaper transformed this obstacle into a PR spot.

Many of the features that characterize the company today were creative responses to financial limitations: re-fillable containers, limited packaging by industry standards, and franchises.

As a successful company, Anita recognizes the responsibility of profit. "I have learned that profit is the lubricant that makes things happen in the marketplace, creates more jobs, and is a legitimate agent for social change. ...It is ... necessary and healthy to make a profit because unless you make the profit, you can't distribute it....One of the joys I get from profits is being able to effect change for the better."[5]

The Body Shop's commitment to all stakeholders is evident in both philosophy and action. Employees who started as salespersons have been supported in starting their own franchises. Products are packaged in recycled paper. A project is in the works in Nepal to make paper from pineapple and banana leaves. The company provides economic support for entire villages in southern India by selling products manufactured by Boys Towns there. Anita states:

> It's sometimes said our people are our greatest asset. People are not an asset. I believe they are the company. People, rather than things, will be the focus of business in the future; ...organizations will have to conform more to the needs of the individual, both inside and outside of the company. ...When we have a new product, we make sure the ingredients can be grown in the third world. ...The kids in the Boys Towns in India planted 5 million saplings with the help of 300 local villagers....It's a wonderful belief that people can take an arid area and make it sing and dance with plants as they have done. It's the sort of thing that we're really proud of.[6]

Co-op America: interdependence and cooperation

Co-op America is founder Paul Freundlich's response to the need to build a bridge between a national network of progressive organizations and a significant population of individuals with progressive values and lifestyles. Founded in 1982 and based in Washington, D.C., Co-op America defines itself as a "nonprofit membership association dedicated to creating an alternative marketplace for socially responsible businesses and socially responsible individuals." Today Co-op America includes 40,000 individual and 400 organizational members boasting an annual income of $1.5 million. Co-op America's products and services range from food, crafts and furniture to health insurance, investment products and a magazine that offers strategies for socially responsible economics.

The following excerpt from a letter which appeared in Co-op America's Winter 1988 catalog illustrates both the vision and the reality of this organic organization. The letter is a photograph of the interrelationship and interdependency of all its stakeholders—customers, suppliers and staff—and how, in working together, everyone can have what they want and need.

Dear Friend,

Without a doubt, *you* are the reason *Co-op America Alternative Catalog* exists. You've told us that you care—about strong communities, about democratic workplaces, about our neighbors in the Third World.

But there's another side to this Catalog: our producers. They care, too—about people like you and me. Instead of putting profits ahead of all else, they are committed first to their ties with the people around them, to their craft, and to working toward making this world a peaceful and productive place.

I'd like to share a letter from one of our producers, the Hummer Craft Works that really sums up how important *you* are to the producers:

"Co-op America has made the difference. Before, we were out here in the middle of nowhere working hard every day just to survive. Although we were doing something good, there was something missing. And that was people.

"Co-op America has given us the push we needed to feel even better about ourselves and our work. Thanks so very much for believing in us. You can count on us to do the best job we can."

We'd like to offer thanks to you on behalf of all of our producers. With you, we are making the dream of a marketplace based on cooperation and justice a reality.

—Denise L. Hamler, catalog director

Bread & Circus:
sustaining agriculture, sustaining life

Massachusetts is fortunate to be the home of Bread & Circus, a chain of wholefood supermarkets that exemplify every aspect of a Gaean organization. The company is built and managed around four cornerstones which reflect the philosophy and commitment of CEO Anthony Harnett: (1) To provide the best customer service in the world, (2) To give dignity and worth to every individual, (3) To do everything to the best of our ability, and (4) To support sustainable agriculture.

Anthony grew up in Ireland. Raised on a traditional diet that included sugar and white flour, Anthony's interest in nutrition was catalyzed by his discovery of macrobiotics while in London. He continued his studies in the United States to study with Michio Kushi and returned to Ireland where he opened a wholefoods store. He later returned to the States where he worked first in Erewhon, Boston's first major natural foods store, and then went on to his own venture, Bread & Circus.

Now employing 650 people with five stores and its own bakery/kitchen, Bread & Circus provides a major outlet for farmers using organic and sustainable farming methods, delivers information and healthy food alternatives to countless customers, and contributes consciously to each community in which stores are located. The company has truly blossomed since 1975 when Anthony started the first Bread & Circus store. He had a strong sense of mission:

> I found something I thought was very powerful (macrobiotic diet and philosophy) and I wanted the world to know that this was something they should do. That enthusiasm and conviction was like a magnet that drew a lot of people who were concerned about food and their own health but didn't have a real sense of what to do. This was a very clear purpose. We knew what the answer was.

Over time, the company's mission matured on a customer level. "Today, we're much more embracing. We feel that diet is a personal responsibility. It's your body. We'll offer you a selection of food and information from which to choose. We'll help you choose, but it's your responsibility."

Anthony's personal commitment has grown on a larger level as well.

> On the bigger level, what drives me is that someone needs to
> do something about agriculture in this country. ...A nation's
> health and future is dependent on its ability to produce food,
> quality food. We're producing food for all the wrong reasons.
> We're producing it fast, inexpensively, with limitless shelf
> lives....What we're doing is destroying the soil, destroying
> the water table, polluting the Earth, and destroying its
> ability to reproduce, all very short-run thinking. ... Unless
> we change the way we farm, we're not going to have a
> country.

Bread & Circus' commitment to its people is as striking as
its commitment to the Earth. As the company has grown, an
environment of freedom and respect for the individual has
been maintained while operating effectively and productively.

> There's no symbol of elitism in the company. ...We have no
> corporate parking spaces. The best parking space goes to
> whoever's there first in the morning. You don't get a special
> anything—unless it's earned by performance rather than by
> position. ...We don't really have any policies and procedures
> manuals. ...We also keep changing things. The bottom line
> is does it work? Does it work for you? Does it work for the
> customers? Does it work for the company? If so, do it.

The Heart and Soul of an Organization:
Purpose, Vision and Values

The Body Shop, Co-op America and Bread & Circus exemplify
organizations built around a clear purpose, vision and set of
values. Purpose, vision and values relate to organizations just
as they relate to individual people. They represent the heart
and soul of the organization, what it stands for, why it exists
and what it's working to achieve. Stated most simply, *purpose*
establishes *why the organization exists*, *vision* examines *how
things could be*, and *values* articulate *what matters*. Some
techniques to work with purpose, vision, and values in organizations may seem similar to the ones we used earlier to
develop purpose, vision, and values for individuals. Nonetheless they are useful in creating and managing Gaean organizations.

Purpose

An organization's purpose is its mission, its reason for being. The purpose can be both practical and lofty. The company my business partner Wynne Miller and I run is committed to creating a workplace that works to support our ultimate goal of creating a world that works. While a mechanistic organization's purpose may be utilitarian—to make money, to be the biggest producer of a particular product—a Gaean organization's purpose incorporates ideals and a sense of social responsibility.

Purpose provides a context for all the activities of the people and the organizations. In this sense it is an umbrella under which everything else fits. Purpose is a common thread that runs through all the activities and layers of the organization, aligning the parts and providing coherence and cohesion.

Purpose provides meaning and direction for the organization as a whole, and the people in the organization. This helps the organization establish its identity and is a basis for choosing what it will and won't do. In this way, purpose provides a screen to filter, evaluate and respond to circumstances and opportunities the organization encounters.

Vision

While purpose, the inner thread that provides connection and meaning, is often intangible, vision enables the organization to translate purpose into doable activities and attainable outcomes. Vision provides a clear, common image of how people want things to be, a basis for determining how the organization can grow or evolve, what results people want to achieve, and what needs to be done to achieve these results. In this sense, the vision serves as a higher order goal and a framework from which more immediate goals and a plan of action can be established.

Vision opens the creative potential of the organization and the people who comprise it, allowing the organization to move beyond the current limits and constraints that so often get our attention. The way things are is not the way things always have to be. Vision asks us to consider what's at the heart of things—what is important and what really matters. If our work and our workplace reflect what matters to us, we feel a part of rather than apart from it. We'll bring more of ourselves to work, feel more committed and work more productively.

In order to illustrate purpose and vision further, here are purpose and vision statements of two organizations whose missions reflect a Gaean management philosophy.

The Schweisfurth Foundation

Munich, West Germany, Dr. Franz-Theo Gottwald, Director.

> *Statement of Purpose* [why the organization exists]: The Schweisfurth Foundation supports approaches toward a holistic and fulfilled life in which work and technology will be better in harmony with nature.
>
> *Statement of Vision* [how things can be]: Interaction between man and nature is influenced primarily through work and technology. It is necessary to reinterpret work and technology and their interrelations to the whole. This can be achieved when work is seen not only as a requirement serving to cover the material necessities of life, but also as a possibility enabling the development and formation of a humanistic way of life.

The Nourishment and Life Project

A management consulting firm in Stockholm, Sweden; Jan Backelin and Goran Wiklund, Partners Banbrytarna.

> *Statement of purpose:* Nourishment and Life* is a project aiming at a transformation of the business world challenging it to give nourishment to a life of well-being for individuals, organizations, society, and the planet.
>
> *Statement of vision:* Our vision is that this is the time when Nourishment and Life turns from a Swedish concern to a global commitment. That committed business people will be mirrors that reflect this sunlight over the earth, giving nourishment and life to individuals and organizations around the world. That they will be the teachers of the spiritual purpose of business, the apostles of the sacred mission of organizations.

---

* The Swedish word for business is *naringsliu* which directly translated back to English is *nourishmentlife*.

Values

Values are at the heart of what an organization stands for, and the common threads that run through the organization. They are shared by the people who comprise the organization and help determine the organization's identity or sense of self. Values may be conscious or unconscious, spoken or unspoken, written or unwritten. They act like a magnet, attracting people (employees, customers, shareholders, suppliers) who share the values of the organization and repelling those who don't.

Values provide a screen for all activities, helping determine priorities—what's important and what isn't, what is right and what is wrong. In this sense, values enable the organization to determine who to work with and who not to and what the nature of relationships will be. Values help define the boundaries of the organization and the people who comprise it.

Whether stated or unstated, an organization's values can be identified through examining practices and operations. For an organization to act with integrity and purpose, vision and values need to be commonly understood, commonly stated and commonly embraced. Commitment to what the organization stands for by all of those involved is essential for actions to reflect values.

The following statements reflect the values of two different organizations—a real estate management/property development company and a magazine.

The Flatley Company

A real estate management and development company in Braintree, Massachusetts, Thomas J. Flatley, president and founder.

> The Flatley company has been built on a solid foundation... from a philosophy that we care. We care about people and the quality of service that we deliver to them each day. In every project that we undertake there is a place for people and a sincere interest in every aspect of their lives—a place where people can live, work, grow up and grow old. A place where the quality of life is high, not just good enough.

Mothering Magazine

This national magazine is located in Santa Fe, New Mexico, Peggy O'Mara, Editor.

> *Mothering* magazine celebrates the experience of mothering and fathering as something worthy of one's best efforts and seeks to inspire a recognition of the immense importance and value of parenting and family life in the development of the full human potential of both parents and children. ... *Mothering* is a fierce advocate of the needs and rights of the child and a gentle supporter of the parents as we strive to empower decision making that will embrace and consider the needs of all members of the family. We explore the reality of human relationships in the family setting, recognizing that raising heirs of our civilization well is the prerequisite for healing it.

Preparing Purpose, Values, and Vision Statements for Your Organization

How can you prepare a statement of purpose, values and vision for your organization? Here is an exercise that will help you unearth your organization's identity, aspirations and goals.

Exercise

Begin by gathering a group of colleagues or co-workers who will answer these questions together. Have each person write his or her ideas individually and then share them with the group.

1. What is the purpose of your organization? Why does it exist?
2. What does your organization stand for?
3. What are you most proud of about your organization?
4. If your organization achieved its highest potential, what contribution would it make?

Record everyone's answers on flipchart pages. Circle key words and look for themes; make a list of both. Use this information to write a mission or purpose statement for the organization. The answers to questions two and three provide the basis for sifting out the organization's values. A clear summary of the group's answers to question four will articulate your vision for the organization.

To develop a strategy for the next year, have the group brainstorm:

1. Where was the organization one year ago?
2. Where is it now?
3. Where do we want it to be one year from now?

Discussing questions one and two provides a framework for discussing question three. Summarizing the group's answers to question three gives you a target or vision for the next year. You can use this statement as a basis for planning. To begin the planning process:

1. Have each person identify three results they would like the organization to achieve over the next year.
2. Record everyone's results on flipchart paper.
3. Choose three to five priorities as a focus for the next year.
4. Explore what is needed to create each of these results by discussing the following questions:
   • What is the current situation relative to this result?
   • What is our desired situation?

Record your answers on a chart under the headings:

Result We Want To Achieve:_____		
Current Situation	GAP	Desired Situation

5. Now explore what needs to be done to fill in the gap, to create your desired situation.
   • What specific actions need to be taken?
   • What resources do you need?
   • What don't you know that you need to know?
   • Where can you begin?
   • What needs to be done before something else can be done?
   • In what timeframe does each step need to be taken?
   • Who in your group can do what?

- How does the list of things that need to be done relate to people's interests and abilities?
- What are your top priorities?

6. From your answers to the above questions, you can identify both *what needs to be done* and *who is interested in doing what*. What's most important is to choose things that people really want to do and can do. Attention can only be focused on a limited number of priorities at once. What will hold the group's attention individually and as a whole are those items that are compelling to you and seem important. This is the basis for preparing a plan of action for the group.

7. As you bring the meeting to a close, make sure you have a list of what next steps are to be taken, who is responsible for each step, who will help see that they get done, and by what date they will be done. Decide how and when you will review progress and identify next steps to be taken.

Starting Where You Are

Whether you work for yourself or in an organization, you can help create the kind of work environment you want by starting where you are. Begin by asking yourself the following questions: What do you like about your organization? Why did you choose to work there? What don't you like, and why don't you like it? If your organization could be its best, how would it be? Considering your answers to these questions, is there anything you want to create or change in your organization that you find compelling? If so, what is it? Those things which compel us are usually those things that move us to act. What can you do about the issue or situation you find compelling? Do you need others to work with you? What can you do right now? What is your first step? When will you do it? Who can support you in doing it?

While you may feel overwhelmed by what you don't know, by the magnitude of what needs to be done or by the insignificance of what you feel you alone can do, focus on what compels you and what you *can* do. Everything that gets done is done one step at a time. Having a friend or colleague you can talk to about your ideas, your questions, your concerns and your progress can help you stay energized. Think about what could happen if every person took one step each day toward creating an organization you all could be really proud of and what it would be like to be with people who are creating an organization that really works. You CAN make a difference starting where you are.

CHAPTER 10

Making Your Mark

I am of the opinion that my life belongs to the whole community and as long as I live it is my privilege to do for it whatever I can... Life is no 'brief candle' to me. It is a sort of splendid torch which I have got hold of for the moment, and I want to make it burn as brightly as possible before handing it on to other generations.

— GEORGE BERNARD SHAW

I have had this quote taped to my refrigerator for five years and have believed these words of George Bernard Shaw ever since I was a little girl. I have always wanted to make a mark—to feel that the world was truly richer and better for my having been here.

Even though I knew I wanted to make a difference, I have often wondered if I could. "The world is so big and I'm so small," I would say to myself. "Is there anything I can do that will really contribute to the quality of life on this Earth? And even if I try, can I do it right? Can I handle the responsibility? I'm not perfect. I have limitations. Sometimes I can't understand why things are the way they are. I get so passionate. I focus on what seems impossible. I get so deeply committed to the vision, I sometimes scare people, I sometimes scare myself." I now realize what I was really questioning was my own worthiness. I always knew what mattered to me; I didn't know that what mattered to me really mattered.

Over time, as I have had the privilege of working with many people committed to finding meaning in their lives and achieving their highest potential, I have come to know that most of us have these kinds of questions. Am I good enough? What can I do? How much of an impact can one person make? What if no one understands? What if I don't do it right? Will I be all alone if I take a stand? Can I bear it? These questions have been asked so many times. Yet even with all our fears and self-doubt, I've come to see that something in our very nature yearns to feel a greater sense of connectedness, to reach out and deeply touch others in a way that lasts. All of us really want to make a mark.

When you acknowledge what really matters, when you live from your convictions, you make a difference quite naturally. I've come to see that the greatest mark is made not by what we do but through who we are. When you live from what matters, what you do is an expression of who you are and what you care about. Every day you touch and enrich people you encounter— at home, at work and even in the supermarket, laundromat or exercise class. You often don't even realize the impact you are having just by being yourself.

In this sense, I've come to understand what service truly means. Service is giving from a sense of love so naturally that you do it without thinking. Service is a natural respect for other people and a genuine response to their needs. Service is different than acting out of your own need to give so that you feel good about yourself; it comes when you already feel good about yourself and so come to others whole and complete. The best foundation I have found for contributing to others, for making a mark, is loving, growing and developing myself. Love is a choice, and the first choice is to love ourselves.

Living with Vision: Making a Difference

There are many people in our society who are touching the lives of others, oftentimes in ways they don't even realize, making the world a better place. Following are the stories of some of those people. While what they do differs, what these people share is a sense of personal vision, the courage to act on their convictions, and a commitment to do what they can to make the world a better place. They all are doing what they can within their own environments and their own limitations, and each is doing it with love and conviction. May we all have the courage to similarly express our convictions in our work and in our lives and may we be supported as we do so.

Charles Hamilton: a commitment to values

I first met Charles Hamilton while I was still in high school. He was president of Charles Hamilton Associates, a consulting firm that had done impressive work in the Brookline, Massachusetts, school system. What struck me on our first meeting, and has stayed with me to this day, was his passionate commitment to human values and his understanding of what it meant to make a difference.

Making a difference is important to Charles. In fact a sign reading "We make a difference" has been hanging in his office for eight years, ever since those words first came to him. "I've always been a maverick," Chuck told me. As a boy and young man he found himself in leadership roles again and again, establishing organizations to eradicate racial injustice, getting elected vice president of the student body in his undergraduate years and moving on to president in graduate school, and becoming the first new graduate elected to the Board of National Association of Social Workers in Chicago. Charles was deeply influenced by his mother's philosophy, "Demand that people respect you" and "You have enough—it's all in your outlook." Having recently turned 50, he has worked for 32 years trying to influence social change by "mobilizing with others" and taking a stand for what he believes in at a local and national level. Charles is also a successful businessman and organizational consultant.

Commitment to fairness and justice has moved Charles to act time and time again.

> In a situation that bases judgments of exclusion or denial on what I label as superficial characteristics, whether gender, race or ethnicity, if I assess there was some unilaterally imposed standard that is not applied equally in my perception to everybody, then my reaction is to immediately become very conscious, to think about what if anything I should do, so I'm not at all indifferent to it....Depending on the nature of the situation and the circumstances of my own life, I will then choose what to do. More often than not, my efforts have been to influence the situation in a more equitable direction.

Charles models what he advocates.

> I place a high value on...trying to live consistently and
> behaving consistently with my own values. If I'm very
> concerned with discrimination against black people, the
> inconsistency would be any basis for discrimination that I
> would be indifferent or inattentive to. It really gets at an
> ideal value set that is very much a part of who I am....I've
> done a lot of things that have improved the social condition
> for people in very concrete ways through my own belief in
> possibilities....It's a way of being. It's compelling. The fact of
> being a black person, which has been exciting for me, has
> contributed to deepening my sense of who I am as a human
> being. We can look at many people over history who have
> made contributions. If we take the label off, we'd just say,
> "That's a fine contribution."

While Charles is able to see possibilities, he is also very
realistic and practical. "It's important not to lose touch with
today's reality—what we're trying to transition out of. A very
compelling motivation for me has been wanting conditions to
be better for my children." His own children have benefited
from the results of his work in the early years with surburban
school systems.

His commitment is to empowering people.

> Everyone has something to bring, to contribute within them-
> selves. Start with these personal assets and then look at
> where you need to grow and develop.

Dick Weiss: respect and compassion for humankind

Over the last five years, I have generated an abundance of
correspondence and have spent a large amount of time in the
Shrewsbury Post Office. While I have known Dick Weiss
primarily in his role as the man behind the counter, I have
always been struck by his ability to make my day. His
knowledge of the postal service and his loving attitude have
made a strong impression.

I am not the only customer who has noticed the presence of
this extraordinary man who describes himself quite modestly
as "an ordinary guy" who "loves life." Walking into the post
office, you can see how many customers are waiting for Dick
to help them.

> I have repeat customers. I have people who won't go to
> anyone else....When the average person comes into the post
> office, he puts his trust in that clerk....The customer isn't
> expected to know all the angles. I do. I'll tell a customer, "You
> can send something this way a heck of a lot cheaper and time-
> wise it will be the same." They appreciate this. They have
> confidence in me.

Having worked at the post office since 1972, Dick sees his
work as helping people. This comes naturally to him.

> I'll go out of my way to help people. That's the way I am. I help
> a lot of people. It's got to be in you. I'd much rather have a
> good friend than money. You can't buy a friend. I've got
> friends all over the world, and I like it that way.

Dick's bond with Shrewsbury is even more striking when
one realizes that he lives out of state, in North Smithfield,
Rhode Island, and commutes over an hour to work every day.

> I have good relationships with people. These people come in;
> they've had a hard weekend. They get up; they hate their job;
> they're going to work anyway; and I know this. I was very
> fortunate. I love my work. And I rib them—and I get a laugh
> out of them. They feel a little better when they go out of here.
> And this is the theory I work on: make people feel a little
> better. This is my contribution. Start 'em off in the morning
> with a smile. It may only last five minutes, but at least it's
> five minutes more than they would have had.

Dick's care for his customers is genuine and constant.
"Some people say I have charisma. I don't see the charisma in
myself. I'm just a natural person who can talk to people." In
being who he is, Dick makes a mark in many people's lives
every day.

John Cutrell: a visionary in the mainstream

So often we think of visionaries as working apart from others
or outside the mainstream. John Cutrell, 51, is an example of
living with vision in a very large, complex, mainstream
environment, the United States government. As Director of
the International Highway Program for the Federal Highway
Administration in Washington, D.C., he agrees with Einstein
that one can't solve today's problems with the same thinking
used to create them.

The role of the visionary in society is to take us to places we haven't been before, creating ways of being that haven't been tried or have been rejected. Most people focus on what's already been tried and didn't work. Visionaries are willing to unshackle their thought processes to go beyond the limits of the now and allow a greater Mind to come into play. The visionary doesn't have to do all the doing. He or she can show what can be done and promote the vision with others, serving as a motivator, as a catalyst. My gift is being able to see beyond the status quo to a new way of working that will create a better utilization of resources.

John feels one can make a difference in a large organization.

We think that creativity can't happen in our large organizations, that we have to be apart from the organization to be creative and totally free. There are so many resources in the mainstream. If the mainstream doesn't work, we can tap its resources, redirect them toward the establishment of a vision, making it work rather than working alone in an isolated grassroots effort. Transforming your organizational context requires seeing it with new possibilities and the potential for change. The world is waiting for things to work better. The reason we don't normally attempt this is fear. It's a misconception and counterproductive to think that people have a real investment in having it not work when they really don't know any better way. They know in their heart things aren't working.

John places a high value on communication and the quality of human relationships.

Visionaries aren't unique. They're able to communicate heart to heart—finding a spark of enthusiasm, lighting a spark in the heart of the other person. The person listening needs to have the opening. When I come from my heart, it affects how the listener can hear. When the other person knows I'm open, when I'm coming from my heart, they're able to unmask and create the opening to their heart so communication can be effective. Looking good and exercising authority masks coming from the heart. I can't come from a place of "I have power over you." When I'm free to be the person I truly am, having the openness to express from my innermost source where things really matter, call it my soul or my creative being, when I don't try to cover it up, then communication can occur. Communication is not only the speaking—it's the way we are.

John sees the government as a vital force in creating a sustainable society.

> Much of what the government is responsible for today is making it work, despite errors in perception. The government's essential purpose is to bring order out of the chaos we create that we're incapable of bringing about ourselves. Government acts as a centralized aggregate conscience. Decentralization is putting the responsibility back into the heart and hands of the people. In the meantime, the government will work when more people who constitute the government operate from the heart. The government is made of a cross-section of society. When these people have the freedom to be what they're capable of being, the government will have breakthroughs commensurate with the breakthroughs at the level of the individual.

Mark Satin: keeping the dream alive

How often do you have a forum to talk about your deepest concerns and hopes for your life, the lives of others, and the state of the world? So many of the "important" things never get said or discussed in conversation, never mind in the media. Mark Satin, 41, recognizes this and through his newsletter, *New Options*, provides an opportunity for a dialogue about what really matters. Based in Washington, D.C., *New Options* is a political newsletter with a concise style and practical focus that in just five years has attracted 10,000 subscribers. Running through *New Options* is a commitment to fairness—looking at the whole picture on an issue and valuing the points of view of all innovative thinkers and activists.

At the heart of political, economic and social issues are usually deeper questions. By presenting differing points of view on a practical issue and exploring the value in all, Mark is able to unearth the deeper questions.

Over time, Mark's vision for *New Options* has become focused and practical. His commitment to building his subscriber base was compelling and, having reached his subscription goal, his commitment to serve them is equally moving.

> When I started out, I literally wanted *New Options* to change
> the world. I don't think *New Options* can do that now. I don't
> think any publication, any written document, can. I think
> only people working together through conflict, working out
> of pain and their passion, can create real change. What I
> think *New Options* does is...keep alive the flame of the
> thousands of people throughout American history who be-
> lieved in concepts like simple living, ecology and decentral-
> ism and being responsible to all the members of the human
> race not just the members of one's own country. If I can find
> 10,000 subscribers who understand on the deepest level
> what I am trying to do in *New Options*, and they use it and
> find that it nourishes their work and they turn to it for guid-
> ance and for information...I would feel perfectly complete.

Most simply, Mark's contribution is to keep the dream
alive—"the dream that's in most Americans' hearts: that we
can live simply, that we can live for each other and not suffer
or hurt ourselves in the process." He intends to convey to
intelligent, caring people that this is not just a pipe dream but
that there are people all over the country who've thought how
this could be done in economics, social policy and international affairs. *New Options* provides real support and builds
many bridges for all its subscribers.

Frank White: communicating possibilities

Frank White, 44, of Newton, Massachusetts, is an author and
consultant whose passion lives in the relationship between
space exploration and human evolution. His gift is seeing
possibilities.

> In just about anything I look at, I see only possibilities. This
> seems to be valuable to other people who only see the limits.
> I can't say I don't see the limits. I just don't consider them
> inevitable.

For Frank, as with many visionaries, having ideas without
sharing them is insufficient.

> Visionaries have an intense need to communicate what they
> see. The point of having an idea is to communicate it. When
> you share a vision, it points out a realistic possibility for the
> future. To share a vision is all you really have to do. A
> powerful vision is non-coercive. I don't need to have any
> power over you to get the vision to happen. All I have to do

is transmit it. That's the way I have power in relationship to you, by sharing the vision. It's voluntary on your part to embrace it.

Frank has taken upon himself to communicate why exploration of outer space is critical to human evolution.

I am sharing the vision of a human space program—a global commitment to space exploration—and am working to show how this approach could be transformational for humanity. My basic approach is to communicate the message in as many media as I can, starting with my book *The Overview Effect*.

Frank recognizes that change happens through the efforts of committed individuals, although the road is not always smooth and comfortable.

The individual is the only entity that makes a difference. Anything important that's ever been done started with an individual's initiative. Sometimes it takes awhile before you get to the point to be willing to do it. The hardest part is feeling you're different from other people—maybe that you're not saying anything— that you're an idealist. You have to trust yourself no matter what anyone else is saying. That's hard.

Karen Sands: empowering other people

Karen Sands, 44, who lives in Manhattan in New York City, has made a difference in a wide variety of environments. Working as a teacher, helping kids "learn how to think while keeping their childish wonder," founding a Women's Center in Summit, New Jersey, building her own jewelry manufacturing and direct sales business, and being a successful intrapreneur in a Fortune 500 financial institution are all part of Karen's story. Whether in the classroom, the community at large, the marketplace or the boardroom, Karen has applied her gift of aligning people around a common goal, turning them on and creating the synergy for them to thrive.

Her venture into the corporate world followed her success as an entrepreneur. "If I'm this effective on my own, what could I do with the resources of a corporation?" she wondered. "I really wanted to prove that if you could build an organization aligned around a vision and mission and tap the potential of every individual, you could produce tremendous business

results and breakthroughs." Seeing an opportunity to respond to changing demands in the marketplace, Karen developed a plan for her company to provide innovative, quality
products responding to customers' needs. When she first
proposed her idea to the Senior Executive Committee and
members of the ranks of middle management, she was greeted
with the response "We've never done it that way before."
Pursuing her vision, she was eventually invited to implement
her plan in another division.

Building a team of 23 professionals, she created a model
working and learning environment. Her management philosophy was:

> Mistakes are opportunities. Tell the truth as fast as possible;
> the only failure is not participating. Everyone in the organi-
> zation—from clerical on up—has a role to play and adds
> value. No one is locked into one role—roles are cross-fertil-
> ized. The whole team has to be a star. Decisions are resolu-
> tions rather than compromises; and unresolved issues or
> conflicts, especially interpersonal ones, have to be addressed
> immediately.

To initiate participative management and team alignment,
Karen conducted a five-day training session for the entire
team including her staff, all vendors, and company members
from interfacing areas. Participants moved during the session
from being strangers to being experts in collaboration and in
bringing products to market. "Lots of time was spent discussing visions and values, exploring what was most important to
them, how to be together and how to work together." Karen's
team produced phenomenal sales, creating breakthrough
business results.

While she was successful at creating a winning climate
within her division, the company was going through political
upheaval. Her group continued to have phenomenal results,
but morale was diminishing. "It felt as though the outer world
was closing in." Her division had been protected until the top
management was cut out. The people who replaced them "did
not understand anything we were doing." Negativity and fear
started destroying the effort. Karen got her people what they
needed and accepted that she had to begin a new phase of her
career. Her management team was gone just three months
after she left.

It was sad to see what we created lost, yet the seeds of vision that turned into flowers are now out in the world producing more seeds and more flowers. We're all a bit cynical about building that kind of visionary organization within a bureaucratic monolith, yet we're optimistic that it can be done if each of us finds the right environment. Our biggest lesson was win-win, empowering, participative management does work to produce long-term, bottom line results.

Karen is now searching to find the next arena in which to make her mark. I have no doubt that wherever she goes, she will be successful.

Making Your Own Unique Contribution

While each one of these stories is unique, they share common threads. Here are questions you can ask yourself as you explore how you can make your own unique contribution.

- What's important to you?
- What do you feel compelled to do? (Most likely that's what's needed)
- What are some of your strongest convictions?
- Think about a situation in the past when you have taken a stand or chosen to act no matter what. What was the situation? What motivated you to act? What did you do? How did you impact the situation?
- What issues are you facing at home, at work or in your community that call your attention? What, if anything, can you do?
- If you look back at your life one year from now, what mark would you like to have made?

Answers to any or all of these questions will help you see where to begin. Respect your own sense of timing; learn what attracts you and what turns you off. While we all want others to love and approve us, there are times when our own convictions will be so strong that what others think won't matter. Too, when you act out of your personal convictions, your own truth, you are loving yourself.

CHAPTER 11

Living on the Earth

Humans must learn to see themselves less as beings separate from the Earth and more as a dimension of the Earth. The well-being of the Earth is the only way to the well-being of the human.

— *THOMAS BERRY*

In an effort to be practical and learn more about what everyone called the *real world*, I took two economics courses in college in addition to my two major study areas—music and psychobiology.

My encounter with economic theory, which viewed life as a big puzzle that could be surgically sliced into many pieces, was less than enlightening. In order to study any one piece of the puzzle, all other pieces had to be held constant. From my own experience, managing resources meant juggling many factors at once. Things change constantly. Who was I to think I could hold anything constant? In economics, the world could be reduced to a series of equations and formulas and what wasn't understood went into a mysterious black box called *externalities*. Reducing life to an intellectual exercise challenged the very fabric of my being.

In graduate school, economics was even more confusing for a person with a sense of social responsibility. One professor was enamored with the term, *bang for the buck*. He talked of *maximizing returns* and *exploiting resources*. While I could recite the rules and principles of economic law, I was unsettled and dissatisfied. Life was not a simple string of cause and effect relationships.

We are taught to manage resources by separation and compartmentalization. As thinking people, we've focused on getting more for less, losing our sense of interconnectedness and cooperation and trading off social responsibility for personal interest. We've built a world on belief in scarcity, which has led to fear and hoarding as we fight to survive. The Earth has suffered and so have we. Having exploited our natural resources and built walls and weapons to protect us from those upon whom we are mutually dependent, our actual global survival is at stake.

Now is the time for everyone to become aware of how we live and how this affects our lives, others and the Earth. We need to find ways of living and working that are sustainable, that recognize our partnership with nature and our responsibility to take care of personal and common resources. Rather than think of humanity as a collection of individuals, we need to think of ourselves as a species, one of many. As we arrive at the conscious/compassionate stage of development, our role as caretakers and conscious/compassionate investors becomes clear. This requires a new economics—one based on the root meaning of the word economics, the management of the resources of our common household, the Earth. In Chapter 9 I called this new approach to economics—which draws its models from nature—Gaean Economics.[1]

Practically, this involves expanding our approach to management and balancing the best aspects of current business practice—results orientation, thinking strategically, collecting the facts, reviewing progress periodically and making adjustments—with qualitative, less tangible and humanistic considerations. The key issue is one of balance and wholism.

Energy: The Most Fundamental Resource

Energy is the clay out of which we craft all life forms. Money, time and personal energy are the three forms of energy we have to manage. Energy can be exchanged, managed and directed yet it needs to keep flowing. When the flow stops, so does life.

Today we often confuse conserving energy with blocking energy. If you are afraid there isn't enough energy to go around, you grab as much as you can and hold on to what you get. While you think you are building a wall of protection in a cold, harsh world, you are in fact building a wall of isolation. When there's a wall, nothing can get in and nothing can get out. The flow is stopped.

Resources and Investment

When we speak of investment, money is usually what we are referring to. But our time and personal energy are also an investment. A man who was planning to set up his own counseling practice asked me what my rates were. I told him I have a sliding scale and a policy that no clients in need would be turned away because they couldn't afford to pay. That's how I give to society.

Return on investment usually means a financial return. The other returns that accompany the investment of any form of energy are not accounted for. Likewise, risk or cost are defined primarily in financial terms, overlooking personal, organizational and environmental risks and costs.

Do we think of investment only in financial terms because money is something fairly easy to quantify? We can touch a dollar bill. The concepts of day, hour, minute and second help us quantify time. Personal energy is the hardest resource to measure. Can you touch or quantify love?

Your Energy

Perhaps the resource you think about least often, and take most for granted, is your own energy. You may not pay attention to your energy level until you are tired, ill or depleted, yet you use your energy constantly in all that you do. Your own energy is your most precious resource, yet in taking it for granted you may act as though it were nothing. When you give energy, you give a person some of yourself. You give someone your energy by thinking and caring about them even when they are not present.

How can you manage your personal energy more consciously? The first step is to become aware that you have it and what it feels like physically. Notice your energy level in the morning, at mid-day and at night. When do you feel energized? Tired? Rested? Do particular people and places replenish or drain your energy? Activities that are fun and important nourish me. Obligations, shoulds and oughts, drain me. As you observe what energizes and what depletes you, determine what changes you can make to feel happier and be more energized.

Choosing a healthy lifestyle is essential to sustaining a high energy level. Good nutrition, plenty of sleep and avoidance of substances such as alcohol, sugar, coffee and nicotine are common sense. Emotional support and spiritual nourishment are as important as the care and feeding of your body. You need to feel loved and connected. When you are emotionally needy, you may feel heavy, empty or blocked. Often we're afraid to ask someone to listen, comfort or just be there when we really need them. Intimate friendships, solid colleagueships and being part of a contributing group or community all provide emotional support. Quiet time alone, meditation, and many kinds of physical activity provide space for inner nourishment. When you keep too busy, you literally don't have the time or space to breathe and you suffocate. At the root of a vital lifestyle is discovering what you really care about. The more you know what matters to you, the more you are able to choose healthy activities, relationships, environments and projects, and the more you can invest your time and energy in productive ways.

Time

Today it seems like there's never enough time. Thinking about time is almost as stressful as thinking about money. Many suffer from *hurry-up disease*, in which you attempt to do everything faster in hopes that you'll avoid being overwhelmed by your list of things to do. The faster and harder you work, the more tired and anxious you get; yet the list of things to do never ends. At the root of the hurry-up-disease is a sense of urgency that comes from being out of touch with your real needs and your natural rhythm. You can't tell the difference between what you *think* you need to do and what you *really* need to do. What you have to do seems impossible, yet you feel compelled to do it all. The race against the clock is addictive. To break free, you need to bridge the split between your head and heart and learn what really matters.

In chasing time, your attention is focused on outside forces. The more dependent you become on external cues, the less attention you give to internal ones. As I chose to become more familiar with my internal time clock, I have become reacquainted with a whole series of sensations and feelings I had ignored under the guise of being "more functional and productive." I have relearned how to eat. I now eat breakfast on a beautiful placemat in my dining room surrounded by morning sunlight, rather than in the car driving to a meeting. I've learned to eat when I'm hungry and not because the clock says it's meal time. At first I was afraid to trust my body for fear I would starve or lose control. My fears have deep roots that had to heal in order to learn this trust. I've learned to live in the present moment without having to prepare for the future or make up for the past. I've learned to ask myself what I really want right now and trust that's all I need to know. You can invest in the present moment. The future provides direction for investing; the past provides insight about what does and doesn't work. Now that I've learned to slow down and relax, managing time is much easier.

What can you do to come to terms with time? Continue to ask yourself: "What really matters?" "What's important?" "What do I really need?" While you may talk a lot about priorities, sorting them out is often difficult. Ask your heart and gut for their opinions as well as your head. Arrange a meeting among your heart, gut and head where they talk out their different points of view. You'll come to a consensus or at least better understand what the tensions are. If you have a things-to-do list, make a shorter list of only what you really need to do today. Use your gut and head in making the list. Are the two lists different? Ask yourself what needs to be done first and what can wait. Focus your energy on what you *can* do rather than on what you *can't* do. Ask yourself what is a reasonable amount to do today? *Over-* rather than *underesti-*

mate the amount of time for a task. Build in leisure time. A key question I ask myself is, "What's my next step?" By defining a next step and taking it, I feel a sense of accomplishment and am healthfully productive.

To become familiar with your internal cues and to learn to trust your body takes time. Become more familiar with your pulse, your heartbeat, your internal timeclock. Notice the difference between being hungry and full. Allow yourself to sleep in for as long as you want on a Saturday morning. Notice how you feel when you wake up. Notice when you feel energized or depleted. Give yourself permission to do what you really want and see how you feel. In time you may discover that you are more in control by being less controlling. You'll feel more relaxed and less stressed out. There's another benefit too: as you learn to manage your own time, you'll be more sensitive and responsive to others' time needs. We have to recognize our own rhythm if we want to cohabit in harmony with the other creatures on the Earth.

Money: Our Culture's Most Loaded Concept

Money is the focus and the foundation of our society. You may feel that money has become too strong a force in your personal life, the organizations you are part of, and the world as a whole. While few would argue that money is a predominant force in our lives and our world today, we rarely talk about it. Few people are totally comfortable with their relationship to money. How often do you find yourself having intimate conversations about this relationship? Thinking about money sends chills up the stiffest person's spine and creates knots in the calmest stomach. Talking about money is a social taboo. Wealthy, poor, or just making ends meet, almost no one is satisfied with their financial position.

Money is our culture's most *loaded* concept, a metaphor for our worst fears, our highest expectations. Money evokes passion in most people. As our society defines it, money and spirituality are separate and almost mutually exclusive. Money is attached to sexuality, power and personal value. The messages society gives us about money are frightening and disempowering: it's dirty (*money is the root of all evil*), you can never have enough (*you can't be too rich or too thin*), it's hard to come by (*money doesn't grow on trees*), and money determines your worth as a person and as a sexual being (*the measure of a man is the bulge in his pants— his wallet*). Most of us don't have an answer to the question, "How much money is enough?"

What Is Money and Why Is It so Compelling?

Objectively, money is only a concept and a resource.

Money is an abstraction, a symbol, "just a piece of paper." In some cultures money is rice, metal, beads or another substance. Money in and of itself has no meaning.

Money is a medium of exchange, a standard or common denominator when you exchange goods and services.

Money is most fundamentally energy, a tool to help you get where you need to go. Because money is energy, when left to its natural rhythm it flows and therefore needs to be channeled and invested.

Psychologically and culturally, money is a mirror. We have projected onto it our most basic needs, our most fundamental fears and our deepest hungers.

Money is power with the ability to influence other people. How people hold and use their power varies. Some choose to manipulate with money. Others choose to serve.

Money is safety and security, enabling you to meet your basic needs for survival: food, shelter and protection.

Money separates people when we differentiate between the haves and the have-nots, the upper class and the lower class, between first world and third world countries. Money causes rifts in families and can throw longstanding friendships into question.

Money is called all those things desired in our heart of hearts: "money is freedom," "money is happiness," "money is respect," "money can bring me peace," and "money is love."

Money is responsibility and for some a burden. Managing this resource takes a great deal of time and energy.

Money is opportunity, an enabler that can open doors.

Money is acknowledgement, a reward for one's labors. In theory money says you are making a contribution and is society's way of recognizing your contribution.

Money is an obsession. For some, no amount of money is enough as they are driven to acquire more and more out of fear or in search of *something* that is missing. The search is one of passion, fury and desperation that can break up marriages, wear down health and still never end. All the money in the world can't fill the void people feel inside; a void that is, in essence, a spiritual one. An obsession with money is an addiction just like that of the alcoholic, the compulsive overeater or the workaholic.

We take money very seriously. Only rarely do people answer, "Money is fun." If money is indeed a mirror for our culture and our times, the message is very strong, reflecting how alienated we are from our deepest values and from others. More and more people are asking, "What is the point of it all? If this is having it all, why do I feel so unfulfilled?"

A Sign of the Times: Our Common Spiritual Void

Whether you have it all, or seem to have very little, you may be familiar with a feeling that something is missing, a kind of hunger or yearning that is intense, fearful and won't go away. These feelings are so uncomfortable and compelling that you feel you would do anything to rid yourself of them. You can locate the feelings in your body—sometimes in the solar plexus, often in the heart. The void or emptiness may reach into your very center, appearing dark and unfriendly when you close your eyes and dare to approach that point. Many use money, food, sex, exercise, work or alcohol to fill the void, only to find it still there. The desperate struggle to fill the void is at the root of the proliferation of addictions in society today.

"Why can't I fill the void? Why won't it go away?" When faced with emptiness, we feel disconnected and alone. What we are truly yearning for is a sense of connection, both with self and others. The emptiness is actually a spiritual void. As thinking people, we have separated and held in opposition our physical and spiritual needs. We have pushed aside our spiritual selves to achieve material prosperity. Individually and collectively we are searching for a sense of self and a sense of our own power. Having lost touch with our natural creative power, we have projected power onto objects and symbols outside ourselves. We have built a society around the myth of separation, carving a deep chasm between the material and the spiritual. The split becomes a vacuum, sucking in whatever is in its path.

I feel that the absence of love and connectedness in our lives and society has created the chasm. Love may be defined in many ways: self-love, love of others, and the love of God. Love is a kind of nourishment that is essential for all of us. When we experience love, we feel full and whole. Life becomes an arena of limitless possibilities. Individually and collectively, we are facing a call toward integration. In searching for a sense of self, you are searching for an experience of connection and living fully. Your desire for connection begins with feelings of emptiness and terror. Accompanying the terror are feelings of helplessness, hopelessness and desperation that eventually force you to surrender to a universal power greater than yourself—call it God, nature, or life itself. As you surrender, a part of you dies, yet a part of you opens. You gain a fuller sense of self, feel connected, and loved. Through opening you receive the spiritual nourishment you need.

Distorted Priorities: Money and the Void

I have always marvelled that in our society the people who have the greatest ability to earn money most quickly are those who work most closely with money. The closer you are to people and human values, the farther you seem to be from the money. Compare the salary of an investment banker with a pre-school teacher. In our high technology culture, financial transactions can be completed in a moment's time without making contact with people or actual currency. Great sums of money can be generated by simply playing electronic games in the stock market, seemingly without providing any concrete service to society.

As I listened to a very successful investment professional speak about the "harsh reality" of the business world, the magic and illusion of money that has led to a state of imbalance in the distribution of resources became increasingly clear. "Our business aims to maximize return on scarce resources," he said. "It's a high pressure culture; it's not healthy, but the people who thrive on it can make a lot of money. They're not happy; they may drink alot, but they're successful." When our lives revolve around money, they become empty and devoid of meaning.

The world of work raises as many questions about what is valued and what really matters as the world of finance. Salary structures within organizations reflect the value society places on an individual's acquired skills. A creative secretary is unlikely to receive the salary or recognition of a successful engineer yet may do more to nourish the life of the company. We are valued for the roles we play rather than for who we are and what we contribute. What we can quantify is valued. To quantify love, care and creativity is more difficult than to count the number of computers manufactured. We measure how much is produced rather than the process of production.

The fundamental fact that people and organizations depend on the interrelationship of all the parts and that a flow and balance between these parts needs to be maintained is ignored. We are taught to separate work from the rest of our lives so that work is rarely a labor of love but more of a burden and an economic necessity. Our most precious resources: our energy, love and creativity are wasted. What a high price we pay for the dollar earned in today's work world.

Natural Economics:
Beyond Scarcity to Abundance

Many of the economic concepts we live with reflect our separation from the natural world—particularly the notion of scarcity that tells us there will never be enough for all. Belief in scarcity threatens survival and leads to fear, greed and hoarding. When left to her own devices, nature offers us abundance. A belief in abundance is inherent in many ancient philosophies and current spiritual teachings. Whether one believes in scarcity or abundance will determine the design, quality and fabric of one's life.

Abundance is a choice to view and embrace each moment as an opportunity for growth and learning and to view life in a larger context.

Abundance is a quality of life, a choice to be open, to move continually toward possibility while clearly seeing the limitations of the current situation.

Abundance allows us to live in each moment, to experience the moment for what it is, empty, full or somewhere in between.

Abundance is filled with tests— situations that challenge your choice to live fully, posing fear, doubt and limits. As you face them, you learn and grow.

Abundance asks you to be true to yourself, to listen to your heart, and to dance in harmony with the rhythm of the universe. In dance, there are times you move forward and times you move away. Through living abundantly, you learn there is a time, a season, for everything.

Living abundantly takes faith. At those moments when you don't know, only inner conviction can help you to follow your heart and continue toward your vision.

Abundance assures you that life will provide whatever you truly need, that everything you need is already inside of you and in the world around you. Learning to listen to your instincts, your intuition and your heart will enable you to find what you need and the resources to fulfill that need.

Abundance helps you learn what "enough" means. Having everything you need is different than being greedy. Greed comes from feeling you can never have enough, and creates an insatiable hunger that can neither see nor respect the needs of other living creatures. Living abundantly includes a respect for self, for others and for all life. Nature has a balance. You need to learn to find this balance in yourself in order to manage the resources you have.

Abundance in action: conscious/compassionate investment

As more and more people are drawn to invest their resources in socially conscious ways, we bump up against the limitations of the existing system for investment. Through the Social Investment Movement we are provided expanded investment alternatives. Social investment funds generally screen out companies investing in South Africa, nuclear weapons or industries that pollute the environment. However, there is a difference between not investing in activities that clash with our values and directly supporting projects fully aligned with our values. Small businesses often provide opportunities and ways to support human values and a positive future, yet for the socially conscious investor to meet the socially conscious small business person is difficult. There is still a ways to go before we can truly put our money where our heart is.

The current financing system with its short-term goals and narrow focus does not address the needs of the practical visionary or the social entrepreneur. Most visions require many kinds of support—money, people's energy and natural resources—over time to be realized. Short-term financial goals squeeze the life out of an evolving vision-based organization. In this sense, today's investment system is limited in its ability to support social evolution.

Perhaps for this reason few businesses today are founded with a primary commitment to social consciousness and global service. Operating to make a difference while making a profit is still a conceptual stretch in business. Great faith and courage are needed to balance service and profit motives. Many of us don't want to risk trying.

As we reach the conscious/compassionate stage in human development, our investment outlook will change. Using our heads and our hearts to consciously develop investment criteria, we will act more fully on our personal values and a common sense of social responsibility. As we better understand our own natures, and regain an appreciation for the natural world we are part of, we will build more wholistic, sustainable organizations. As we realize that investment is about how we use our personal energy and time as well as our money, investment will take on a whole new meaning.

Value-based investment

As you become clearer about your personal values and your own sense of worth, you can help create a new system that I call *value-based investment*. In value-based investment you invest your money, time and energy in what you care about, focusing on what you want to create and how you want it created. When investing—your time, energy or money—you consider how your actions impact and are impacted by the Earth, being practical about what you need to receive in return for your investment. This leads to a new set of criteria to evaluate business opportunities. Investing all our resources consciously at personal, organizational and planetary levels, we can create and support the planet's evolution as well as those organizations whose values are based on respect for people, and the planet will likely cause them to be most successful in the long run.

Your Own Sense of Value

In order to know where to place your money, your time and your energy, you need to know what really matters to you and how you would act out of what matters. The following exercise provides an opportunity to explore what value means to you, and how you would define your own sense of value.

Exercise

Get into a comfortable position, close your eyes, and take a deep breath. Give yourself enough space to breathe, letting air come in through your nose as you inhale, moving down your throat, filling your belly, providing nourishment and support to all the cells of your body. Let each cell take in just the right amount of nourishment and support in its own time and its own space. And when each cell feels complete, let the nourishment and support you provide return back out through your mouth as you exhale, returning back to the source from which it came, only to have it return back to you once again with your next inhalation, as the circle of your breath is complete. Take a moment to become familiar with the circle of your breath and the circle of nourishment and support it provides and you provide.

Whenever you feel ready, see if you can find your heart, your physical heart, beating in your chest, your pulse beating in your arms, in your hands—wherever you feel it. Take a moment to become more familiar with your heart, your pulse. When ready, ask your heart, "How would I define my sense of value?" Now, let your heart respond in its own time, in its own way. Acknowledge your heart and its response.

Next, allow your focus to move to your gut, and take a moment to notice where your gut lives in your body and how it feels right now. When you're ready, ask your gut, "How would I define my sense of value?" Let your gut respond in its own time. Acknowledge your gut and its response.

Allow your focus to move to your head, and take a moment to notice where your head is located and how it is feeling. Whenever you feel ready, ask your head, "How would I define my sense of value?" Let your head respond in its own time, in its own way. Acknowledge your head and its response.

Now, revisit your heart, your gut, and your head, and ask your whole self the question, "How would I define my sense of value?" Take a moment to notice your response. Then, very slowly and gently, take a deep breath and bring your focus back into the room.

On a piece of paper draw pictures representing the responses of your heart, gut, head and whole self. Make notes about how you would define your sense of value.

The Resources of the Earth

Most of us take the resources of the Earth for granted. To do so, however, is becoming more difficult. We've acted without considering how our actions affect the environment. For many years we've lived as though the Earth were an endless supply closet and waste receptacle. Of course, this is not true. The damage we humans have done to the Earth—to her water, air, trees and the atmosphere surrounding the planet—has reached a crisis proportion. As the Earth suffers, we suffer. Nothing lives in isolation. The Earth is a living organism of which we are part. Individuals, organizations and nations can no longer act without considering how our actions affect the Earth. Each of us has personal responsibility to care for the Earth, to consciously manage her natural resources.

Living on the Earth:
guidelines for conscious resource management

Here are some guidelines for contributing to the quality of life on Earth:

Recognize that everything begins with the individual. The

way you manage your own resources provides a model for others.

Learn what it means to love yourself. You are important and deserve to be cared about. Taking care of yourself may involve healing, as all of us are wounded in some way, as is the Earth. As you heal yourself, you begin to heal the Earth of which you are part.

Become more aware of the environments in which you live. Your home, the organizations you work in, society, as well as the Earth, are all environments. You are a caretaker in your environment, as well as a part of it. Live in partnership with your environment, considering the needs of the whole as well as your own needs.

Learn what matters to you and what you need. Learn to know yourself intimately. Take risks. Look inside and consider your own truth as you look at the world around you. The better you know yourself, the more you are able to define your part in the larger scheme of things.

Imagine you are part of an evolutionary direction that is greater than all of us. As we move from the painful myth of separation to the experience of partnership and connection with ourselves, others, and the Earth—conscious, responsible resource management will become easy and natural.

Building a Sustainable World

As we journey from adolescence to adulthood as a species, and move from separateness to interconnectedness, we will reawaken to the organic relationship between individuals, organizations and nature. How different we will feel as our lives are clearly purposeful, as we feel a strong sense of self and a sense of connection to others and the Earth. How much richer we will be as we are able to serve and profit from our service, no longer having to separate work from the rest of our lives. As we recognize that organizations can provide bridges between person, community and planet we will take care of their health and well-being. As we reconnect with our own nature— bridging the split between mind and body, reclaiming the power of the heart—we will become more aware of the natural world around us and the place we have as caretakers of the

Earth. Socially conscious education will become more highly valued as we recognize that the future of our world lies in our hands and the hands of our children. We are being called together to do our part and collaborate to build a sustainable world.

Choosing Your Vision

Fundamentally, living with vision is a choice. There are times when none of us can know what the future will bring, what is ultimately right, or what the risks and rewards actually are. Many times I've faced the darkness and had nothing to hold on to but my vision. I've been afraid and chosen my vision nonetheless. I wrote a song about fear and how it can keep me from living with vision, but when I close my eyes, take a deep breath, acknowledge the fear and move on, I am okay. As I have faced my fear, my sense of self and my faith have grown stronger. While I am not free from fear, I now understand that it is one of vision's companions—as are love, joy and peace. Choosing to live with vision is choosing to experience everything. Following is a verse to the song I wrote called "When Dreams Suffer":

> *In our lives none can escape*
> *Obstacles, worries and fears,*
> *They can consume*
> *They can deter*
> *They can compromise our lives.*
> *Holding on, yet letting go,*
> *Trusting that time will fulfill*
> *Your truest needs*
> *Your deepest dreams....*

Writing this book has felt like writing a letter to a close friend, opening my heart and letting the words pour out. We've shared a lot as we've moved through the pages of *Living With Vision*. I wish you the courage, strength, and support to hold fast to your dreams and to celebrate the inner peace and joy that are yours as you experience what it means to be fully alive.

Acknowledgements

This book reflects the love and attention of many people who have contributed to its evolution and my evolution. Its roots are in my childhood where Virginia Thompson, my grammar school principal, made a mark. Her strength and conviction helped me build a solid foundation for taking my place in the world.

Rick Levine played a crucial role in my unfoldment, being there for me after the attempt on my life and always reflecting back to me who I truly am. Ellen Ober provided sisterhood and guidance as she opened the door for my journey into the corporate world. Bill Steul has always recognized my vision, its place in business and in the world at large. The late Kaleel Jamison once told me, "you are wasting your life," as she weighed my corporate position with my creative ability. I now understand what she meant. Fran Meline, my partner in the Life Integration Trainings, introduced me to Hakomi body-centered psychotherapy which has proved to be an important building block for my work. Jenny, a wise tabby cat, was my soul's companion for 16 years.

My therapy and consulting clients, each participant in the Money, Work and Personal Purpose workshops, Life Integration Trainings, and other seminars I have facilitated and the people I've met at a multitude of conferences—have all touched me and taught me. Thanks to all of the people who sent me their visions when this book was *Visions for A Positive Future*, and the community of friends and colleagues who sent me to the Florence Convocation where I realized I had to write this book.

Martin Leith, Eileen Conn, Mark LeDoux, Michael Jaro, Linda DeHart, Catherine Cooper, Jan Backelin, Lynne Lockhart, Bob Holder, Frank White, Nancy Allen, Joan and Wil Hastings, Sheryll Hirschberger, Roger Pritchard, Theo

Gottwald, and Monica, Joe, Vicki and Evy at the New Road Map Foundation have each provided a blend of colleagueship, love and support. This book could never have been without Pat Wagner who connected me with Knowledge Systems, and Jim Ritscher who connected me with my editor, the book's skilled and loving midwife, Marie Cantlon. Thanks to each of the people whose words and stories appear in *Living With Vision*; your words have helped me weave a rich tapestry.

Thanks to all who have read the manuscript as it evolved, in particular, Susan Meeker-Lowry, Annie Gill, Caroline Neville, Jim Ritscher, and Rosalind Fritz. Margo Schmidt deserves particular recognition for both her careful review and insightful contributions to the manuscript. Rose LeBeau's author's photo helps express the book's message. Mirtala has contributed to my evolution in countless ways. Thanks to David Speicher and Carolyn Aleksic at Knowledge Systems for bringing this book to the world.

Closest to my heart are Peter Stroh—without whom much of this book could not have been written, Jamie Wedell—whose care, insight and strength have deeply enriched my life, Tony Cifizzari—whose friendship has nurtured my spirit and my heart, Susan Meeker-Lowry—a soul sister with a common mission in Gaean Economics, and my two other soul sisters, Lisa Wexler and Rosalind Fritz—who have always been there for me. My deepest appreciation goes to my business partner, Wynne Miller, whose gifts of friendship and collaboration are abundant and infinite. Her patience, compassion and honesty as this book took me on a powerful journey, sometimes away from our business, exemplify committed partnership.

Thanks as well to the many people who have touched me along my journey and those who are yet to touch me in the days to come. Thanks to my family for bringing me into this world and to God for giving me the opportunity to live fully and offer what I have with joy and passion.

Chapter Notes

Chapter 1

1. Robert Theobald's model for the Compassionate Era from *The Rapids of Change*, 1987, has contributed to my thinking about man's relationship to nature from an evolutionary point of view.

2. The relationship between knowing, understanding and wisdom is a contribution from Margo Schmidt, colleague and consultant.

3. From a booklet on "Projects and Perspectives" published by the New Road Map Foundation, Seattle, Washington.

Chapter 2

1. From "Reclaiming the Spirit of Healing" by His Royal Highness, Charles, Prince of Wales in *The Heart of the Healer*, edited by Dawson Church and Dr. Alan Sherr, p. 9.

2. From a speech given by Martin Luther King on August 28, 1963 during the Civil Rights March on Washington, D.C.

3. Excerpt from a June 1988 article in the *Boston Globe* about Rising Tide by Jeff McLaughlin.

4. From an interview with Norman Cousins by Jane Barrash in the *Continuum Center Newsletter*, volume 1:2, Spring/Summer 1988, published by the Continuum Center, Minneapolis, MN.

Chapter 3

1. Hans Selye, *The Stress of Life*, Mc-Graw-Hill, New York, 1986.

2. This exercise comes from the Money, Work and Personal Purpose workshops developed by Linda Marks and Wynne Miller, The Marks-Miller Collaborative.

3. Structural tension is described in *The Path of Least Resistance* by Robert Fritz, DMA, Salem, MA, 1984, and in the course he has developed, Technologies For Creating™.

4. This exercise also comes from the Money, Work and Personal Purpose workshop.

Chapter 4

1. Michael Ray speaking at "The Heart of Business," a one-day seminar featuring prominent business thinkers exploring the relationship between material success and pursuing the "Path of the Heart."

2. From *Hearts That We Broke Long Ago* by Merle Shain, p. 31.

3. © 1987 Carolyn Treadway. Reprinted from Pilgrimage Magazine

Chapter 5

1. I would like to acknowledge the contribution Margo Schmidt has made to this section and this chapter. Her thoughts and ideas have deepened and enriched the content presented here.

2. Incorporates ideas on personal and social change from the Life Experiences Model, Knowledge Systems, Inc., 1987.

3. This model of current reality, desired reality, and the gap is found in organization development theory for the management of change, and in DMA, the work of Robert Fritz.

Chapter 7

1. Taken from a presentation by Carolyn Estes at the 2nd North American Bioregional Congress in Traverse City, MI, August, 1986.

2. This particular technique draws upon what I have learned from Hakomi body-centered psychotherapy. Hakomi is a gentle and powerful approach to therapy, respecting the many different realms as well as the whole of the human organism. This technique helps you bridge the split between mind and body and do deep, lasting work that enables fuller self-expression and greater integration.

3. Excerpted from "Integrating Spirit and Work," an article I wrote in 1986 that appears in *New Visions For Our Work, Our Organizations and Our World*, a self-published collection of about 20 articles.

Chapter 8

1. Danaan Parry, the founder of the Earthsteward's Network and the Holyearth Foundation, lectures and teaches on conflict resolution around the world.

2. Excerpted from an interview with John-Richard Turner in *Sources, The Baltimore New Age Magazine*, Spring 1987. Other comments based on "The Possible Relationship," an article written by the UV Family which appeared in the Summer 1985 issue of In Context magazine.

3. From an article in the *Loveland Daily Reporter Herald*, March 10, 1982.

4. "The Spiral of Relationship" is a poem I wrote © 1987.

Chapter 9

1. The material presented here originally appeared in *The Gaean Business*, Gaean Voices, Summer 1987, © 1987 Linda Marks.

2,3. A profile of Anita Roddick is included in *Intrapreneurship* by Ronnie Lessem, Wildwood House, London, 1987.

4, 5, 6. These comments were drawn from Anita's talk, "The Responsibility of Profit," given at the "From Organisation to Organism" conference held at the Findhorn Foundation, October, 1987.

Chapter 11

1. In 1986 Susan Meeker-Lowry and I with a group of other colleagues founded the Institute for Gaean Economics. Contact IGE at 64 Main Street, 2nd Floor, Montpelier, VT 05602. Susan and I are currently developing a model fro comparing traditional and Gaean organizations (discussed in Chapter 9).

APPENDIX

Resources for the Reader

Books

Ackoff, Russell L., *Creating the Corporate Future: Plan or Be Planned For*, John Wiley, 1981.

Adams, John D. , ed., *Transforming Work*.Miles River Press, 1984; also *Transforming Leadership*.Miles River Press, 1986.

Bass, Ellen and Laura Davis, *The Courage to Heal*.Harper and Row, 1988.

Bentov, Itzhak, *Stalking the Wild Pendulu:On the Mechanics of Consciousness*. Dutton, 1977; also, with Mirtala Bentov, *A Cosmic Book:On the Mechanics of Creation*.Dutton, 1982.

Borysenko, Joan, *Minding the Body, Mending the Mind*.

Bridges, William, *Transitions: Making Sense of Life's Changes*, Addison-Wesley, 1980.

Capra, Fritjof, *The Tao of Physics*, Bantam, 1977.

Cheatham, Annie, and Mary Clare Powell, *This Way Daybreak Comes:Women's Values and the Future*.New Society Publishers, 1986.

Choices and Connections, The First Catalog of the Global Family, Human Potential Resources, Inc., 1987; also, *Choices and Connections '88 - '89: Resources For Personal Growth*, 1988.

Church, Dawson and Dr. Alan Sherr, ed., *The Heart of the Healer*, Aslan Publishing, 1987.

Dass, Ram and Paul Gorman, *How Can I Help?* Knopf, 1985.

Devall, Bill and George Sessions, *Deep Ecology: Living As If Nature Mattered*, Gibbs M. Smith, 1985.

Dossey, Larry *Space, Time and Medicine*; also, *Beyond Illness*.

Ekins, Paul, ed., *The Living Economy:A New Economics In the Making*. Routledge and Kegan Paul, 1987.

Elgin, Duane, *Voluntary Simplicity*, Bantam, 1981.

Ferguson, Marilyn, *The Aquarian Conspiracy*, Tarcher, 1980.

Fritz, Robert, *The Path of Least Resistance*, DMA Press, 1984.

Fromm, Erich, *To Have or To Be?*, Bantam, 1981.

Fuller, R. Buckminster, *The Critical Path.*, St. Martin's Press, 1982.

Gendler, J. Ruth, *The Book of Qualities*. Turquoise Mountain Publications, 1984.

Gendlin, Eugene T., *Focusing*. Bantam, 1981.

Gibran, Kahlil, *The Prophet.*, Knopf, 1927, 1983.

Harman, Willis, *The Global Mind Change*, Knowledge Systems, Inc, 1988; *An Incomplete Guide to the Future*, Norton, 1979; also, with Howard Rheingold, *Higher Creativity: Liberating the Unconscious For Breakthrough Insights,* Tarcher, 1984.

Hay, Louise L., *Heal Your Body.*, Hay House, 1982.

Henderson, Hazel, *The Politics of the Solar Age: Alternatives to Economics,* updated edition Knowledge Systems, Inc., 1988; also, *Creating Alternative Futures: The End of Economics*. G.P. Putnam's Sons, 1978.

Houston, Jean, *The Possible Human: A Course In Extending Your Physical, Mental and Creative Abilities*. Tarcher, 1982.

Illich, Ivan, *Medical Nemesis*, Pantheon, 1976.

Jaffe, Dennis T. and Cynthia D. Scott. *Take This Job and Love It*, Simon and Schuster, 1988.

Jamison, Kaleel, *The Nibble Theory.*, Paulist Press, 1984.

Kanter, Rosabeth Moss, *The Change Masters: Innovation for Productivity in the American Corporation,* Simon and Schuster, 1985.

Kidder, Tracy, *The Soul of a New Machine*, Little, Brown, 1981.

Kiev, Ari, *Active Loving,* Bantam, 1979.

Kubler-Ross, Elisabeth, *On Death and Dying*, Macmillan, 1970.

Kurtz, Ron, *Hakomi Therapy*, The Hakomi Institute, 1983; also, with Hector Prestera, *The Body Reveals*, Harper and Row, 1976.

Lessem, Ronnie, *Intrapreneurship*, Wildwood House, 1986.

Lipnack, Jessica and Jeffrey Stamps, *The Networking Book: People Connecting With People,* Methuen, 1986.

Lovelock, J. E., *Gaia: A New Look at Life on Earth*, Oxford University Press, 1979.

Lynch, James J., *The Broken Heart: The Medical Consequences of Loneliness*, Basic Books, 1979.

Marks, Linda, *New Visions For Our Work, Our Organizations and Our World,* 1986.

Maslow, Abraham, *Toward a Psychology of Being*, 2nd ed., Van Nostrand, Reinhold, 1968.

McLaughlin, Corinne and Gordon Davidson, *Builders of the Dawn: Community Lifestyles in a Changing World*, Stillpoint, 1985.

Meeker-Lowry, Susan, *Economics As If the Earth Really Mattered: A Catalyst Guide to Socially Conscious Investing*, New Society Publishers, 1988.

Naisbitt, John, *Megatrends: Ten New Directions Transforming Our Lives*, Warner, 1983.

Parry, Danaan and Lila Forest, *The Earthstewards Handbook*, Sunstone Publications, 1987.

Peace Pilgrim, *Steps Toward Inner Peace*, Friends of Peace Pilgrim.

Peck, M. Scott, *The Road Less Traveled*, Simon and Schuster, 1978.

Pelletier, Kenneth, *Mind as Healer, Mind as Slayer*, Dell, 1977.

Peters, Thomas J. and Robert H. Waterman, *In Search of Excellence: Lessons From America's Best Run Companies,* Warner, 1984.

Phillips, Michael and Salli Raspberry, *Honest Business*, Prentice-Hall, 1981.

Pierrakos, John, *Core Energetics*, Life Rhythm Publications, 1987.

Rako, Susan, M.D. and Harvey Mazer, M.D., *Semrad: The Heart of a Therapist,* Aronson, 1983.

Riegel, E.C., *Flight From Inflation: The Monetary Alternative*, The Heather Foundation, 1978.

Robertson, James, *Future Work: Jobs, Self-Employment and Leisure After the Industrial Era*, Universe Books, 1985.

Rubin, Lillian, *Intimate Strangers*, Harper and Row, 1983.

Russell, Peter, *The Global Brain: Speculations on the Evolutionary Leap to Planetary Consciousness*, Tarcher, 1983.

Sale, Kirkpatrick, *Dwellers In the Land*, Sierra Club Books, 1985.

Schmookler, Andrew Bard, *Sowings and Reapings,* Knowledge Systems, 1989; *The Parable of the Tribes: The Problem of Power in Social Evolution,* Houghton-Mifflin, 1984.

Serinus, Jason, *Psychoimmunity and the Healing Process*, Celestial Arts, 1986.

Selye, Hans, M.D., *The Stress of Life*, McGraw-Hill, 1976.

Shain, Merle, *Hearts That We Broke Long Ago*, Bantam Books, 1983.

Sheldrake, Rupert, *In Context: A New Science of Life,* Tarcher, 1983.

Siegel, Bernard, *Love, Medicine and Miracles*, Harper and Row, 1986.

Spretnak, Charlene and Fritjof Capra, *Green Politics: The Global Promise*, Bear & Co, 1986.

Starhawk, *Truth or Dare*, Harper & Row, 1987.

Swimme, Brian, *The Universe Is A Green Dragon*, Bear & Co, 1984.

Thatcher, David, *Earthrise: A Personal Responsibility*, Foundation House Publications, 1987.

Theobald, Robert, *The Rapids of Change: Social Entrepreneurship In Turbulent Times,* Knowledge Systems, Inc., 1987.

Walsh, Roger, M.D., *Staying Alive: The Psychology of Human Survival*, New Science Library, 1984.

Wiseman, Ann Sayre, *Dreams and Symbolic Healing*, Ansayre Press, 1987.

White, Frank, *The Overview Effect: Space Exploration and Human Evolution*, Houghton-Mifflin, 1987.

White, Robert, and Koichi Shimazu, John Jones, Yoshiaki Nagashima, *One World One People*, ARC International Ltd., 1984.

Newsletters and Magazines

Action Linkage Networker
5825 Telegraph Avenue #45
Oakland, CA 94609

Brain / Mind Bulletin,
P.O. Box 42211
Los Angeles, CA 90042

Building Economic Alternatives
2100 M St., NW, Suite 310
Washington DC 20063
    Published by Co-op America.

Business Dynamics
Box 964, 100 Mile House
British Columbia,
Canada VOK 2EO
    Integrating forces in the
    world of business.

Catalyst: Investing In Social Change
P.O. Box 364
Worcester, VT 05682

Common Boundary
7005 Florida St
Chevy Chase, MD 20815
    Boundary between psychology and spirituality.

Creation
P.O. Box 19216,
Oakland, CA 94619

EastWest
P.O. Box 6769
Syracuse, NY 13217
    Journal of natural health
    living.

Forum for Correspondence and Contact
 International Center for Integrative Studies
45 West 18th Street
New York, New York 10011
    Dialogue on contemporary
    and future issues.

Human Potential Magazine
 5 Layton Road
 London N1 OPX, England.

In Context
P.O. Box 2107
Sequim, WA 98382
    Explores human sustainable
    culture.

Insight
OAL Research Publications Ltd
Cleanjohn House, 90 Ladipo St.
Matori, P.O. Box 9802
Lagos, Nigeria
    A magazine for spiritual
    development.

The Letter Exchange
P.O. Box 6218
Albany, CA 94706
    Magazine for letter writers.

Many Hands
Beyond Words Bookshop
Thorne's Market
Northampton, MA 01060
    Resources for personal and
    social transformation.

Mothering
P.O. Box 8410
Santa Fe, NM 87504
    Mission statement in Chap-
    ter 9.

New Options
Box 1932
Washington DC 20036
    Editor Mark Satin is profiled
    in Chapter 10.

One Earth
The Park
Forres IV36 OTZ, Scotland.
    Findhorn Foundation
    magazine.

Realistic Living
P.O. Box 140826
Dallas, TX 75214
    Journal of ethics, religion.

Spirit of Change
17-8 Thayer Pond
North Oxford, MA 01537
    Resources for total well-
    being.

The Sun
412 West Rosemary Street
Chapel Hill, NC 27514
    A magazine of ideas.

TRANET
Box 567
Rangeley, ME 04970

Woman of Power
P.O. Box 827
Cambridge, MA 02238

Projects and Organizations

Action Linkage
5825 Telegraph Ave, #45
Oakland, CA 94609
    Network of social entrepre-
    neurs.

Beyond War
222 High St.
Palo Alto, CA 94301
    Grass-roots educational
    project, with 10,000 volun-
    teer staff, which encourages
    personal initiative and re-
    sponsibility based on: war is
    obsolete; we are one; work-
    ing together we can build a
    world beyond war.

Briarpatch Network
1514 McGee St.
Berkeley, CA 94703
    Support network for socially
    responsible small businesses
    in Alameda and Marin coun-
    ties, California.

Community Capital Bank
P.O. Box 404920
Brooklyn, NY 11240
    Will be a full-service that
    will lend to small businesses
    and developers to create low
    and moderate income neigh-
    borhoods in New York City.

The Continuum Center
1313 5th St. S.E.
Minneapolis, MN 55414
  Non-profit organized to
  explore the nature of human
  consciousness and our limitless capacity to learn, to be
  well and to care for others.

Co-op America
2100 M St., NW, Suite 310
Washington DC 20063 U
  This organization is profiled
  in Chapter 9.

The Earthstewards Network
P.O. Box 10697
Bainbridge Island, WA 98110
  Network of individuals committed to creating more
  holistic, loving, sharing relationships with each other
  and with all life forms, including our planet itself.

John E. Fetzer Foundation
9292 West KL Avenue
Kalamazoo, MI 49009
  Encourages research, education, and service that seeks
  the integration of physical,
  mental, and spiritual dimensions of experience.

*The Foundation for Community
Encouragement*
The 1900 Building, Suite 202
1900 North Winston Rd.
Knoxville, TN 37919

Friends of Peace Pilgrim
43480 Cedar Ave.
Hemet, CA 92344
  Peace Pilgrim was a woman
  who walked for peace from
  1953 until her death in 1981.
  Her simple message: "This is
  the way of peace: Overcome

evil with good, falsehood
with truth and hatred with
love." Materials include
audio and video tapes of
talks, a booklet and book.

Gesundheit Institute
2630 Walker Place
Arlington, VA 22207
  Model health care community.

The Giraffe Project
Box 759
Langley, WA 98260
  Initiated by Ann Medlock
  and John Graham. By telling stories of "ordinary"
  people doing extraordinary
  things in service to their
  fellow beings, the Project's
  mission is to inspire people
  to stick their necks out for
  the common good.

*Global Cooperation for a Better
World*
866 United Nations Plaza
Room 582
New York, NY 10017
  Focus on creativity and coop-
  eration at grassroots leader-
  ship and professional levels.

Global Family
540 University Avenue, # 225
Palo Alto, CA 94301

Jean Houston's Mystery School
Dromenon, Box 3300
Pomona, NY 10970
  "It's my 20th century version
  of an ancient and honorable
  tradition, the study of the
  world's spiritual mysteries. I
  weave together sacred psychology, music, history, thea-

mind and spirit, and to apply
that knowledge to the ad-
vancement of health and
well-being for humankind.

Interface
552 Main St.
Watertown, MA 02172
New England's center for
programs exploring mind,
body and spirit.

Intertalk
3610 West Sixth Street, # 537
Los Angeles, CA 90020
A non-profit corporation
which promotes a neutral
second world language,
esperanto.

*International Women's Writing
Guild*
Box 810 Gracie Station
New York, NY 10028

The Marks-Miller Collaborative
785 Centre Street
Newton, MA 02158-2599
Consulting and training organization which applies
Gaean business principles to
offer new tools for making a
difference while making a
profit. Offers Money, Work
and Personal Purpose
workshops.

New Road Map Foundation
5557 38th Ave., N.Ee
Seattle, WA 98105
Nonprofit educational
corporation working to
create 'new road maps' for
navigating through life in
two ways: 1. Provides education in skills and techniques
for assuming personal

responsibility for positive
changes in self, family, community, country and world,
and 2. Distributes program
proceeds to other nonprofits
with a similar mission.

*NorthAmerican Bioregional
Congress (NABC)*
P.O. Box 104
Eureka Springs, AR 72632
Major convening of represen-
tatives of the continental bi-
oregional movement.

Office for Open Network
P.O. Box 9845
Denver, CO 80209
A great way to locate peole,
projects and resources.

*Omega Institute for Holistic
Studies*
Lake Drive Rd 2, Box 377
Rhinebeck, NY 12572

*Organization Transformation
Network*
P.O. Box 285
Auburndale, MA 02166
Innovative new ideas for
transforming businesses and
other organizations so they
become vibrant, energized
and alive—and extremely
effective in fulfilling their
objectives.

Planet Drum Foundation
Box 31251
San Francisco, CA 94131

Planet Earth Foundation
1914 North 34th Street, #500,
Seattle, WA 98103
Public education, through
the media, on world issues.

*Organization Transformation
Network*
P.O. Box 285
Auburndale, MA 02166
Innovative ideas for transforming organizations so
they become vibrant, energized and alive—and ex-
tremely effective in fulfilling
their objectives.

Planet Drum Foundation
Box 31251
San Francisco, CA 94131

Planet Earth Foundation
1914 North 34th Street, #500
Seattle, WA 98103
Public education, through
the media, on world issues.

Seva Foundation
108 Spring Lake Drive
Chelsea, MI 48118
International network sharing a dedication to relieve
suffering and recognizing
that human compassion is
the basis of service.

Social Investment Forum
711 Atlantic Avenue
Boston, MA 02111

*The Other Economic Summit
(TOES)*
P.O. Box 4024
Portland, ME 04101
International forum for "new
economics in the making."

The Whole Health Institute
4817 N. County Rd. 29
Loveland, CO 80537
Network of men and women
actively participating in the
healing arts. Concerned with
whole-person health care,
the causes of health, and
extending a healing influence in the world.

Windstar Foundation
Box 308
Snowmass, CO 81654
Conference center for the
investigation of major
planetary issues.

Music and Tapes

Songs From the Heart
Alliance

Buskin and Batteau
Buskin and Batteau

Songs of Friends and Struggle
Bill Milford and Barbara
Siftar

Good Company Productions
(Rising Tide, Marienne Kre-
itlow, Peggy Morgan and
Bette Phelan, Abraham's
Seed, Marian Streetpeople,
Christopher Rowan)

Dreams and Themes
Linda Marks

Midwestern Heart
Claudia Schmidt

Songwriter
Margie Adam (Olivia Rec-
ords)

The Changer and the Changed
Chris Williamson (Olivia)

Turning It Over
Meg Christian (Olivia)

Windham Hill Records
(George Winston, Wil Acker-
man, et al.)

Index